1970

This book may be kept

ON BEING CREATIVE

And Other Essays

ON BEING CREATIVE
And Other Essays

BY

IRVING BABBITT

BIBLO and TANNEN
NEW YORK
1 9 6 8

Τὸ πρῶτον οὐ σπέρμα ἐστὶν ἀλλὰ τὸ τέλειον.

ARISTOTLE, *Metaphysics*, 1072[b].

PREFATORY NOTE

THE essay in this volume on *The Primitivism of Wordsworth* contains the substance of three lectures given at the University of Toronto on the Foundation established by his old students in honor of Professor William J. Alexander. I desire to express my appreciation of numerous courtesies extended to me during my stay in Toronto, especially by Principal Malcolm W. Wallace of University College.

The essay on Julien Benda is taken from my Introduction to the translation of his *Belphégor* (Brewer, Warren and Putnam). I wish to thank the publishers of this work for permission to reprint. The essay on Coleridge appeared originally in *The Nineteenth Century and After*; that on Dr. Johnson in *The Southwest Review*; that on *The Critic and American Life* in *The Forum*; the essays entitled *On Being Creative* and *Romanticism and the Orient* in *The Bookman* (New York). I have made a few additions and omissions in order to adjust the essays to one another. I have not, however, eliminated all repetitions. My excuse for them, so far as there is any, is that they may serve in some small measure to dissipate certain current confusions on the subject of humanism.

I. B.

CAMBRIDGE, MASSACHUSETTS
March, 1932

CONTENTS

INTRODUCTION

THE connecting theme of these essays is found in the Aristotelian dictum[1] that I have taken as my epigraph with its implied disapproval of what we should term nowadays the genetic method. For some time past there has been an interest in origins rather than in ends far beyond anything with which Aristotle was familiar. According to Nietzsche, the German has a predilection for everything that is 'damp,' 'obscure,' and 'evolving.' This predilection, far from being exclusively Teutonic, has been so universal that it has put its stamp on an entire epoch. We are still living in what may be termed a primitivistic movement. Certain persons in the past, especially certain poets, have toyed with primitivistic fancies, but it is only within the last two centuries, at least in the Occident, that primitivism has set up as a serious philosophy of life and threatened the overthrow of humanistic and religious standards.

[1] Literally rendered: ' The first is not the seed but the perfect.'

[xi]

INTRODUCTION

In his attack on traditional standards the primitivist takes as a rule his point of departure in some form of the contrast between the 'natural' and the 'artificial.' More, however, than an insistence on this contrast is needed to make a full-fledged primitivist. Certain Greeks, especially during the post-Socratic period, worked out an opposition between 'nature' (*physis*) and 'convention' (*nomos*) at least as radical as anything achieved in modern times. As a rule, however, the Greek did not, even in the extremity of his revolt from convention, cease to be rationalistic. When he finally abdicated his pride of reason, so far as he did abdicate it, it was not before emotion or instinct or the like, but before the divine will proclaimed by Christianity. In short, to put the matter psychologically, the 'natural,' as conceived by the Stoics and other ancient rationalists, tended to give way to the supernatural in the form of grace.

The surrender to the subrational has, on the other hand, been very marked in our modern movement. If all that the opponent of the 'return to nature' needed to do was to reaffirm the claims of reason, his task would be a comparatively easy one. But behind the problem of the reason, there lurks a far more formidable problem — that of the will. A difference of opinion is possible as to what is most fundamental in traditional Christianity. Many would accord this supreme and central place to the dogma of the Incarnation. One may perhaps affirm on strictly theological grounds that grace underlies even the Incarnation; inasmuch as it was by the grace of the Father that the Son was sent. If we consider the problem from the psychological rather than the theological angle, we are led almost inevitably, as I have just suggested, to put prime emphasis on grace.

One must admit that grace does not appeal in the psychological or any other sense to those who have entered into the naturalistic current that has been running with increasing force since the Renaissance and has become in our day well-nigh irresistible. The individualist of the naturalistic type has not only discarded grace but along with it the whole notion of a transcendent will. In short, he does not grant that man needs to be humble. Those who are convinced of the unsoundness of this attitude may simply repudiate individualism and revert to a purely traditionalist attitude — the attitude that is usually associated, at least in matters of faith and morals, with the Roman Catholic Church; or again he may, like Mr. P. E. More, seek to steer a middle course between a traditional authority in religion that has become so absolute as to be oppressive and the mere anarchy of private judgment.

My own attempt to solve the problem of standards is, as readers of my previous volumes are aware, distinctly different. At the risk of seeming unduly repetitious, I am going to recapitulate the main argument developed in these volumes, first, because it is hardly fair to assume that all my present readers are familiar with this argument, secondly, because it has become apparent that it is in certain respects in need of further elucidation.

I am seeking, then, here and elsewhere to defend what I would define as a positive and critical humanism. The aim of the humanist, and that from the time of the ancient Greeks, has been the avoidance of excess. Anyone who sets out to live temperately and proportionately will find that he will need to impose upon himself a difficult discipline. His attitude towards life will necessarily be dualistic. It will be dualistic in the sense that he recognizes in man a 'self' that is capable of exercising control and another 'self' that needs controlling. The opposition between the two selves is well put by Cicero, one of the most influential of occidental humanists. 'The natural constitution of the human mind,' he says, 'is twofold. One part consists in appetite, by the Greeks termed *hormé* ("impulse"), which hurries a man hither and thither; the other is reason, which instructs and makes clear what is to be done or avoided; thus it follows that reason fitly commands and appetite obeys.' [1]

The primitivist seeks on various grounds to get rid of this dualism. Thus, according to Rousseau, man is 'naturally good.' If evil appears, it is to be referred not to a failure on the part of the individual to control himself but to 'institutions.' In that case, it may be asked, why not simply reaffirm, by way of reply to Rousseau and other sentimental naturalists, the humanistic dualism in much the form in which Cicero stated it? Why complicate the situation by bringing in a discussion of grace, a purely religious problem? I have expressed the opinion on more than one occasion that there has been a serious

[1] *De Officiis, Lib. I*, c. 28.

INTRODUCTION

omission in our modern attempts to construct sound philosophies of life — something that may turn out indeed to be the keystone of the arch. It may be that more is required, if we are to make good this omission, than simply to reassert 'reason' in the Ciceronian sense. A comparison may be of help at this point between occidental humanism and the great tradition of the Far East that is associated with Confucius. According to Hegel,[1] the occidental will find nothing in Confucius that has not been said, and better said by Cicero. There is, however, an idea to which Confucius gives a central place and which is almost entirely absent, not only from Cicero but from Aristotle, who may be considered, doctrinally at least, as the most important of occidental humanists — the idea, namely, of humility. It is hard to distinguish between a humanism, like that of Cicero, which does not go beyond reason, and Stoicism. This more or less stoical humanism has entered as an element, often as the dominant element, into many noble lives; yet the reason that has the support of a higher will, that is, in Confucian phrase, submissive to 'the will

[1] As quoted by J. E. Spingarn.

[xvi]

INTRODUCTION

of heaven,' would seem better able to exercise control over the natural man than a reason that is
purely self-reliant. At all events, it is this higher
will that I have in mind when I raise the question
whether something has not been omitted in our
modern philosophies of life that may turn out to be
the keystone of the arch. Now the assertion of this
quality of will has been almost inseparably bound
up in the Occident with dogmatic and revealed
religion. The higher will has been identified with
God's will, its operation with the doctrine of grace.
In that case, it may be urged, if the humanist seeks
support in something higher than reason, he must
needs turn to Christian theology. I have no
quarrel with those who assume this traditionalist
attitude.[1] At the same time I am unable to agree
with those who deny humanism independent
validity, who hold that it must be *ancilla theologiae*
or at least *religionis*. One has to face the fact, an
unfortunate fact perhaps, that there are many men
of good will for whom dogmatic and revealed
religion has become impossible. Are they therefore
to be banished into outer darkness where there is

[1] Cf. *Democracy and Leadership*, pp. 316-17.

wailing and gnashing of teeth? What has at bottom undermined dogmatic and revealed religion is the growth of the positive and critical spirit. My own somewhat limited programme — for I am not setting up humanism as a substitute for religion — is to meet those who profess to be positive and critical on their own ground and to undertake to show them that in an essential respect they have not been positive and critical enough. The point may perhaps be best illustrated in connection with contemporary psychology. On the pretext of being fully experimental, the psychologist has come to be almost entirely concerned with the subrational and animal sides of human nature. It seems, indeed, to be taken as self-evident that psychology is a purely naturalistic subject; so much so that in some institutions of learning, it has been divorced from the department of philosophy and annexed to that of biology. It is possible, however, to conceive of a humanistic or even a religious psychology that is in its own way experimental or experiential. Though the higher will in man is not amenable to the methods of the laboratory, it may nevertheless be asserted as a primordial fact — something of which

INTRODUCTION

one is immediately aware. This awareness, to be
sure, exists in very different degrees in different individuals, so that one encounters in purely psychological form the equivalent of the mystery of grace.
If one undertakes to define positively the higher
will, one cannot perhaps hit upon a better phrase
than that devised by Mr. Walter Lippmann to
describe the belief that the modern man has tended
to lose — the belief, namely, that 'there is an
immortal essence presiding like a king over his
appetites.' This 'immortal essence,' so far as it has
bearing on actual conduct, means the imposition of
limits on the expansive 'lusts' of the natural man.
The modernist has sought to identify this act of
self-limitation, concentration, and selection — the
human act, par excellence — with mere contraction
and impoverishment, with what William James
terms 'wintry negativity.'

How, it may be asked, does the modernist who is
unfriendly to the idea of an 'immortal essence,'
and in general to the idea of an inner principle of
control set above the temperamental self, propose
to avoid the evils that have always been associated
with unrestraint? I would preface my reply to this

question by quoting a sentence from *Democracy and Leadership*: 'What is disquieting about the time is not so much its open and avowed materialism as what it takes to be its spirituality.' This sham spirituality, as one may say, will be found to consist in a sort of subrational parody of grace: so that even the humanist who does not feel the need of going beyond a Ciceronian dualism will need to take account of the doctrine of grace and its counterfeits, if he is to understand the situation that has grown up since the eighteenth century in connection with the rise of primitivism or emotional romanticism. Professor Arthur O. Lovejoy has maintained that there is no such thing as a single romantic movement during this period but only romanticisms, each one of which needs to be carefully discriminated from the others. I am, on the contrary, ready to maintain with all the emphasis of which I am capable that there *is* a single romantic movement which culminates, so far as the traditional disciplines are concerned, in an opposition, variously conceived, between the idea of imitation and that of spontaneity. Out of the idea of spontaneity grows in turn the notion of 'creativeness,' still dominant internationally, with which I have sought to deal in the title essay of this volume. A still more important aspect of the gospel of spontaneity that has also assumed many forms in many lands is the assumption that one may achieve by a subrational overflow of feeling the 'love' that has been associated traditionally with superrational will in the form of grace. At this essential point primitivism may be regarded as a Christian heresy. I have sought to deal psychologically rather than theologically with the whole problem in several of the following essays, especially perhaps in the essay on Wordsworth.

If I am positive in my mode of affirming the higher will and humanistic in that I am primarily concerned with the bearing of this will on the mediatory virtues, in what sense do I seek to be critical? In brief, one needs, I hold, to be critical if one is to solve on the terms imposed by the modern spirit the problem of standards. The person who yields to his temperamental urges is wont to oscillate from one extreme to the other. 'For me,' said Rousseau, the temperamentalist par excellence, 'there is no intermediary term between

INTRODUCTION

everything and nothing.' If any one sets himself
the humanistic task of achieving the intermediary
term between extremes, he will find that it is not
enough to exercise an inner check on temperament,
he will need to exercise this check intelligently; and
to exercise it intelligently he will need to look up to
some norm. Norms and standards have been very
much associated in the past with the absolute in
either its metaphysical or its theological form; so
that anyone who sets out to defend standards is at
once suspect of absolutism. Thus Mr. Santayana
concludes triumphantly what is meant in part
apparently as a refutation of my own position:
'Absolutism smells of fustiness as well as of fag-
gots.' ¹ Absolutism may not be quite so sinister
as Mr. Santayana supposes, but in any case my
withers are unwrung. My endeavor has been to
show that, even if one dispenses with absolutes, one
may still retain standards.

I hope that, especially at this point, where it is so
hard to avoid misunderstanding, I may be allowed a
good deal of repetition and recapitulation. Strictly
speaking, I have said, life does not give here an ele-

¹ *The Genteel Tradition at Bay*, p. 74.

ment of oneness and there an element of change: it gives a oneness that is always changing. Moreover, man does not contemplate this oneness from without: he is himself a oneness that is always changing. Now it is a psychological fact that the changeful element both in man himself and in the outer world is closely associated with the sense of illusion: so that the most critical report on life in the whole of English literature is perhaps that of Shakespeare: 'We are such stuff as dreams are made on.' The world, however, did not have to wait for Shakespeare to learn that life is dreamlike and illusory. This is a topic that has been much enlarged on throughout the ages and is not in itself especially edifying. The rôle that many Hindus assign to *māyā*, for example, would seem altogether inordinate. The early Buddhists are more satisfactory than most other Hindu philosophers on this point, not only because they deal more psychologically and less metaphysically with the idea that life is a dream, but also because they are more definite as to the nature of the true awakening. The very word Buddha means the Awakened. Compared with the founder of their faith, the rest of us, if we are to believe the Buddhists, are mere somnambulists. One is reminded of a saying of Goethe: 'Error stands in the same relation to truth as sleeping to waking.' In that case the genuineness of one's awakening will be in direct ratio to one's apprehension of the truth. As to the difficulty of any such apprehension there are still many who are in sympathy with Pontius Pilate. One may, however, make certain broad distinctions regarding what may be understood by the truth. 'Ye shall know the truth,' we read in the Gospel, 'and the truth shall make you free.' A truth that makes one free is at all events not the truth of the behaviorist. On the other hand, there is a certain psychological agreement between Christian and Buddhist, however far apart they may be theologically, as to the nature of truth: they both include in their truth, for example, the belief in a higher will and make freedom depend, though it must be admitted in very different ways, on the activity of this will.

Truth, humanistic as well as religious, so far as it involves the assertion of a specifically human quality of will, has evidently been compromised not only by the primitivists of whom I have spoken, who have

[xxiv]

set up a sort of subrational parody of it, but by the mechanists and determinists who have virtually denied it. Many observers look on the latter class as more dangerous than the former. The essential problem today is, they hold, how to escape from the excess of mechanism, whether one understand by mechanism the mechanizing of mind itself or the multiplication of machines in the outer world. I am not convinced as to the soundness of this view. There would seem to be no harm in man's gaining control of the forces of nature — and the mechanistic hypothesis has been a powerful aid to this end — provided he does not in the process lose control of himself. The primitivist undermines the principle of control in more insidious fashion than the mechanist. He not only sets up dubious substitutes for the traditional disciplines, but often assails the scientific intellect itself, even to the point of falling into obscurantism. No one indeed is wont to make louder lament over the triumph of mechanism than the primitivist.

The tendency of science to overstep its due boundaries and so to run into pseudo-science is none the less a serious evil. Much of the prestige now enjoyed by the man of science can be shown to arise from a fundamental confusion of categories. People look to him for illumination on subjects on which, merely as a man of science, he is no more qualified to speak than the ordinary person. They listen, for example, to a debate between Messrs. Millikan and Eddington on the question whether the universe is or is not 'running down,' as though this debate had a deep religious significance. The man of science himself often enters into the illusion. Thus an eminent physicist writes of certain recent bewildering developments in his subject that these developments must not be taken to mean that science is baffled; they may mean, on the contrary, that it is on the point of discovering the Godhead. One should, to be sure, beware of speaking too absolutely; one should not, for instance, deny all validity to the so-called argument from design in either its older or its more recent form. The eighteenth century deist saw behind the phenomena of nature a sort of divine watch-maker. Sir James Jeans infers from his searching of the heavens that God is rather a super-mathematician.

Nevertheless one may say in the words of the

INTRODUCTION

Imitation — and that without a particle of obscurantism — of certain efforts now being made to
wrest from Nature her more recondite secrets:
'Why dispute about hidden and obscure matters
for our ignorance of which we shall not be re-
proved at the Judgment?' One suspects the more
ambitious of the scientific theorists of attempting to do something that Pascal, himself an eminent
man of science, declared to be impossible —
namely, to grasp either one or both of the two
'infinites' — the infinite of largeness and that
of smallness — by which man is encompassed.
But even though the science be genuine it is
largely irrelevant, as Pascal again has pointed
out, in the realm of specifically human values.
One can scarcely repeat too often his distinction between the three orders — first, the order
of material nature, second, the order of mind,
third, the order of charity. To this last order
alone he applies the epithet supernatural; it transcends at all events the proper domain of physical
science.

The tendency of physical science to presume
beyond its due bounds can be traced to a certain

usurpation on the part of reason — a particular form of the triumph of pride over humility. If one admit a higher will at all, one must grant at the same time that the rôle of reason in its relation to this will is not primary but at most instrumental, that reason cannot hope to formulate finally what is by definition above it. I have already pointed out another respect in which life baffles the mere rationalist: its unity and its diversity are indissolubly blended — only another way of saying that its reality is indissolubly blended with illusion. Try to separate the unity and the diversity too absolutely, as the rationalist is always tempted to do, and one falls either into a metaphysic of the One or a metaphysic of the Many. Western philosophy is largely a rather unprofitable record of the clashes between these two types of metaphysicians. One must therefore conclude that it is reasonable not to be a rationalist.

Those who make exaggerated claims for physical science are as a rule rationalistic rather than genuinely positive and critical. A reporter of the Paris Figaro recently interviewed an eminent astronomer as to the relative importance of poetry and science. The astronomer dismissed poetry with disdain on the ground that it is mere illusion whereas science gives 'truth' and 'reality' (apparently purged of all illusion). This attitude, though still common, is not exactly that of the most recent type of speculative scientist. Eddington, for example, is so ready to recognize the rôle of illusion, even in science, that, if some of his statements were taken at their face value, one would have to conclude that scientific 'truth' is scarcely to be distinguished from it. Eddington, however, is not only in danger of slipping into a dubious mysticism, but offers no criterion for discriminating between such truth as may be attained by the man of science and other types of truth — for example, the type aimed at by the humanist.

While repudiating the absolute and exclusive claims of science to truth and reality, one must grant that it has established by soundly experimental methods that there is a constant element in physical nature, even though it is not possible to disengage this element completely from contingency. Similarly one may hope to establish, if not experimentally in the narrower sense, at least experientially that there is in human nature something that abides through all vicissitudes. I have sought to show that anyone who proceeds positively and critically in the realm of human values and at the same time hopes to achieve standards which, without being absolute, are still far from being merely illusory, must seek to coördinate rightly in himself two powers: on the one hand, a power which I term imagination that reaches out and seizes likenesses and analogies; secondly, a power which may be termed analytical reason that discriminates and tests this unifying activity of the imagination, not with reference to any theory, but to the actual data of experience.

The standards thus obtained may be pressed into the service of what I have termed a purely Ciceronian humanism. The humanistic virtues — moderation, common sense and common decency — have often been achieved on these lines in the past and may very well be so achieved in the future. If one goes further and undertakes to deal with the primitivistic parody of the 'order of charity' and in general with the problem of the higher will, more delicate questions evidently arise. To deal adequately with these

INTRODUCTION

questions one needs, we are told, the support of dogma and revelation. I have no quarrel, as I have said, with those who take this position, though holding that it is possible even here to proceed positively and critically.

The most weighty argument that has been advanced for the belief that humanism is likely to prove ineffective save in subordination to Christian orthodoxy is that this orthodoxy can alone supply our modern life with the central purpose it so plainly lacks. That the elimination of the teleological element from life has been in almost direct ratio to the decline of traditional religion is beyond question. The scientific naturalists have been especially unfriendly to what is known in philosophy as final causes. This unfriendliness can, to be sure, be traced in part to the indiscreet use of final causes not only by certain orthodox theologians but by the deists of the eighteenth century. The issue is at all events one that must be faced by every serious thinker. When Aristotle (to return to my epigraph) gives the primacy to ends over origins, he has in mind the supreme and perfect End itself. He conceives of this end of ends as an 'unmoved Mover.'

INTRODUCTION

Mr. P. E. More has pursued Aristotle implacably for having thus put at the center of his cosmic scheme not a personal deity but a metaphysical abstraction. One may ask whether the unmoved Mover is a mere abstraction. Wordsworth, looking forth on the face of nature, seemed to himself to sense a 'central peace, subsisting at the heart of endless agitation.' In his less theological days Mr. More himself found the idea of the unmoved Mover realized in the Greek sculpture of the best period, with its suggestion of vital motion on a background of equally vital repose. So far as the unmoved Mover is only a metaphysical abstraction one must grant Mr. More that it is a poor substitute for a conscious and purposive deity. Nevertheless one may raise the question, especially if one is aiming only at the humanistic virtues, whether it is necessary, in order to restore the teleological element to life, to start with dogmatic assertions about God and the soul rather than with psychological observation. Moreover, if one extend one's historical survey, as one should, to include the Far East, one discovers that not merely the humanistic but the religious virtues have been achieved there on very

INTRODUCTION

different postulates from those that have obtained
in the Occident. One encounters, for example, in
Buddha what must seem to the occidental one of
the strangest of paradoxes: he makes no place for
God in his discipline and denies the soul in the
sense that has usually been given to that term in
both East and West. At the same time he sets up
an ideal of saintliness approximating very closely to
that of the Christian. Furthermore, it is difficult to
study the ancient records without being convinced
that Buddha and many of his early followers were
not in theory merely but in fact saintly. In a recent
essay Mr. More admits as much, but ends by comparing Buddha to a man who has raised a stately
flight of stairs that leads nowhither — perhaps the
most perfect image of pathetic futility ever devised
for a great religious teacher. His essay raises in an
acute form the question whether one's religiousness
is to be measured by the degree to which one brings
forth the 'fruits of the spirit' or by one's theological
affirmations. If one maintains that the theological
affirmations are a necessary preliminary to bringing
forth the fruits, early Buddhism (not to speak of
other non-Christian faiths) supplies evidence to the

contrary. If I had indeed to give an opinion, I should say, with a full sense of my own fallibility as well as of the prodigious difficulty of holding the balance even in comparisons of this kind, that Buddhism has had as many saints as Christianity and that it has, moreover, been less marred than Christianity by intolerance and fanaticism.

Perhaps I scarcely need add that I am not myself speaking as a Buddhist or urging the occidental to abandon his own religious traditions for Buddhism. Renan maintained that one could not be polite in a Parisian omnibus without violating the rules of the company. Even so anyone who set out to be a Buddhist today would find himself in conflict with some of the underlying assumptions of our civilization. To be sure, something similar might be said of anyone who set out to be a Christian. The idea of renunciation which is central in both Christianity and Buddhism is becoming more and more alien to the occidental modernist. There is in general an opposition between the oriental and the occidental view of life — and genuine Christianity has in it a strong oriental element — about which I have spoken more fully in the closing essay of the present volume.

INTRODUCTION

There would seem to be needed at present, as an offset to other forms of mobilization with which we are threatened, a mobilization of the sages. This mobilization should of course be preceded by a close scrutiny of the quality of the recruits. On the other hand, one cannot afford to display a merely dogmatic exclusiveness. Mr. More, who seems to me to have displayed something of this exclusiveness in his recent essay on Buddhism, wrote admirably many years ago, apropos of the culture of ancient India, that we should acquire a knowledge of it, not in order that we may call ourselves 'disciples of Buddha or believers in Brahma,' but that we may 'fortify our individual life with the virtue and dignity of experience.' This is the spirit in which one should study the Far Eastern background in general. A fact that seems to emerge from this ampler survey of the experience of the race is that one may get humanistic and even religious purpose into one's life without indulging in ultimates and absolutes after the metaphysical fashion of Aristotle or the theological fashion of traditional Christianity. One may well come to agree with certain great Asiatics, in contrast at this point with the European intellectual, that the good life is not primarily something to be *known* but something to be *willed*. There is warrant for the belief that if a man *acts* on the light he already has the light will grow. As for the final stages of the path that thus opens progressively, I for one should be content to say with Cardinal Newman, though not perhaps in quite the sense he intended:

> I do not ask to see
> The distant scene — one step enough for me.

Anyone who seeks like myself to draw for wisdom on such diverse sources, East and West, may be accused of falling into an undue eclecticism. An eclectic philosophy is, as a rule, a thing of shreds and patches. I would reply by distinguishing with Goethe and others between an eclectic philosophy and an eclectic philosopher. A philosopher who is not in this late age of the world highly eclectic may justly be viewed with suspicion. It is related that someone inquired of Buddha, shortly after his illumination under the Bo-Tree, who had been his teacher. Buddha replied: 'I have conquered all, I know all, in all conditions of life I am free from taint.... Having by myself attained supernatural

knowledge, to whom can I point as my teacher?'
Anyone who used such language nowadays might
turn out to be another Buddha. The chances would,
however, be at least a million to one that he was a
candidate for the psychopathic ward. Wisdom is
finally a matter of insight; but the individual needs
to assimilate the best of the teaching of the past lest
what he takes to be his insight may turn out to be
only conceit or vain imagining.

Perhaps I may best illustrate what I mean by
being rightly eclectic in connection with this very
problem of the imagination. In dealing with this
problem it seems to me desirable to bring a Socratic
idea into relation with a Buddhistic one and then to
use the two ideas thus combined in defence of an
idea that is central in Christianity. It will be
observed that the contrast I seek to establish in this
volume and elsewhere is not that set up by the neo-
classicists and taken over from them by the romanticists between reason and imagination, but between
different qualities of imagination. When two meanings thus lurk in one word with a resulting peril of
confusion Socrates and his art of inductive defining
must at once be invoked by anyone who aspires to

be critical. This Socratic art is important in its application to all general terms, if it be true, as John Selden averred, that 'syllables govern mankind.' The importance of its application to the term imagination in particular should be manifest if one associates the saying of Selden with a saying attributed to Napoleon: 'Imagination governs mankind.'

The imagination, I have said, reaches out and seizes likenesses. One may thus, without attaining to anything absolute, establish certain constant factors in human experience, provided the likenesses seized by the imagination be properly tested from the point of view of their reality by the power in man that discriminates. Now the 'nature' to which the primitivist would return has not, I maintain, been properly tested in this way and so remains largely a conceit or vain imagining. The primitivist would seem to be especially chimerical when he makes of his 'nature' the basis of fraternal union among men. There appears to be a confusion here between the subrational and the superrational, a confusion that is closely connected with a confused use of general terms. I point out in my essay on Benda that such terms as 'heart' and 'sentiment' undergo, in passing from Pascal to Rousseau a radical transformation; they still refer in Rousseau to something immediate but there the resemblance ends. When Pascal speaks of 'heart,' he means as a rule the illumination of grace and the closely related 'order of charity'; when Rousseau speaks of 'heart,' he means, as a rule, expansive feeling. As is well known, Rousseau's appeal to the heart is a part of his protest against the dogma of original sin. I hold no brief for this dogma, yet there is evidence that the discarding of it has meant the loss of something so essential that on its recovery in some form may hinge the very survival of our civilization.

Let us ask ourselves what difference it makes practically whether one understand the word 'heart' after the fashion of Pascal or after that of Rousseau. The illumination of grace that Pascal associates with the heart evidently involves an inner activity or working of a kind that is absent from the heart of Rousseau. It is at this point that I would bring a Buddhist idea to the support of my Socratic dichotomy of the word heart and so use it as to justify psychologically the element of truth in the dogma of original sin. The distinction I have in mind is that between the man who is spiritually energetic and the man who is spiritually slothful. The equivalent of this distinction is also found in Christianity. The distinction is likewise invaluable for anyone who seeks to solve the humanistic problem — how, namely, to avoid the indolence of extremes.

It would appear from the Socratic and Buddhistic scrutiny I have been attempting of the word heart that 'love' in the religious sense is not something into which one slips passively and temperamentally but is the result of the activity of a higher will. One may of course go further, as Christian orthodoxy requires that one should, and make certain theological affirmations about this will. My own purpose has been fulfilled if I have shown how one may, without venturing beyond psychological observation, be rightly eclectic in the defense of something that is essential in Christianity.

Some indeed, as I have already remarked, would have the humanist confine himself to the problems that arise in connection with his own task of moderate, sensible and decent living, and not thus encroach on the domain of religion. My reply is that the chief adversary of the humanist at present is the humanitarian 'idealist.' Though this type of idealist often usurps (in the United States at least) the name of humanist, he is at bottom not so much pseudo-humanistic as pseudo-religious. The true humanist, for example, agrees with Cicero that justice, adequately defined, must take precedence of all other virtues in the secular order. The humanitarian idealist would give this primacy, not to justice but to peace, a primacy that actually belongs to it only in the religious life of the individual. Does anyone suppose that when Dante says 'His will is our peace' he means peace of the same quality as that which is to be established (in theory) by a super-committee at Geneva?

As a rule the humanitarian idealist sets up as a 'liberal.' Here again it is feasible to press a Socratic dialectic into the service of Christian truth. 'Where the Spirit of the Lord is,' says Saint Paul, 'there is liberty.' Speaking again not as an orthodox Christian but simply as a psychological observer, I am unable to discover much of the 'Spirit of the Lord' in the liberty of the typical modernist. It would seem important in dealing with the idea of liberty as in dealing with that of love to distinguish between the spiritually supine and the spiritually strenuous. Rousseau says that he based 'an indomitable spirit of liberty' on 'an indolence that was beyond belief.' There is too much of this subtle psychic indolence from which Rousseau suffered in the whole liberal movement that has been under way for several generations. Its chief concern has been with throwing off rather than with taking on controls. Carlyle has described in his picturesque phrase liberalism of this sort as an unstrapping of the devil. He represents the crowd as shouting in ecstatic chorus at each successive emancipation from control, 'Glory, glory, another strap is gone!' Carlyle's own programme for strapping up the devil would seem dubious for reasons that may be very briefly stated. In the first place, the 'hero' to whom he would have us ordinary mortals subordinate ourselves is more remarkable for the vigor of his outer working than for the inner working to which everything that is specifically human in man is finally related. In the second place, Carlyle disparages Socratic self-knowledge, some degree of which would nevertheless seem needful if one's working, either inner or outer, is to be intelligent. That Carlyle was right, however, in deeming modernist liberty dangerously one-sided is indubitable. Things extreme and one-sided have a way of running ironically into their opposites. Many liberals of the modernist type both here and abroad are now looking for their 'liberty' to Moscow! The modernist movement has many merits: but in so far as it has encouraged men to surrender their imaginations to ill-defined general terms (beginning with liberty itself), one may say of it, as Burke said of the French National Assembly, that its improvements are superficial, its errors fundamental. As a result of this weakness of the movement on the side of definition, 'ideals' have been professed which, judged even from the point of view of the social benefits at which they aim, turn out, when put to the test, to be largely illusory; judged from the point of view of the inner life of the individual, they are found to make neither for humanistic poise nor again for the peace of religion. I have sought to show in the following pages that the first step in dealing with 'ideals' of

[xliii]

this kind is, unless indeed one is content to be a pure traditionalist, to submit them to a criticism far more incisive than any now discoverable among our intellectuals.

ON BEING CREATIVE
And Other Essays

I

ON BEING CREATIVE

THE recent debate on humanism supplied ample
evidence that the 'great confusion,' predicted by
Sainte-Beuve, is now upon us. Though the confusion is European as well as American, in this
country it may be said to be worse confounded.
Greater havoc has been wrought here than in
Europe by the new education, an education that
has been concerned with anything rather than with
the transmission of 'the best that has been thought
and said in the world.' As a rule it is only by the
assimilation of this 'best' that one may hope to
build up critical standards. The impression one got
from the humanistic debate was that our critical
standards have suffered even more severely than
had been suspected. It would be possible to com-
pile from the utterances of the anti-humanist critics
a pendant to the amusing skit by Pope and others
on the Art of Sinking in Poetry. Outstanding examples of the Art of Sinking in Criticism are Mrs.

[1]

ON BEING CREATIVE

Mary Colum's assertion that Aristotle's literary taste, as revealed in the *Poetics*, was of the kind we associate with the tired business man — the kind that inclines 'to good detective stories and melo-drama'; also the assertion of Mr. Edmund Wilson that the characters of Sophocles have no more ethical substance than those of Mr. Eugene O'Neill.[1] One is justified in speaking of a cultural collapse when critics can make such assertions without at once being brought to book by a considerable body of readers. In its extreme form the denial of standards has amounted to a repudiation of the two chief traditions of the Occident, the classical and the Christian. According to Mr. Fausset,[2] all orthodox and 'official' Christians have been wrong in their interpretation of Jesus; according to Mr. Henry Hazlitt, anyone who makes a plea for decorum must be a Caspar Milquetoast. Even those who allow a place for the religious and humanistic virtues in life hold that they are irrelevant in art and letters; here creative genius should have unim-peded sway. Some of the chief points at issue,

[1] See *The New Republic*, March 19, 1930, p. 115.
[2] See his volume, *The Proving of Psyche*.

[2]

indeed, between humanist and anti-humanist converge upon this idea of creation. According to their opponents, the humanists are sterile souls who seek to dam up the spontaneity of the true artists and force them back into the pinfold of the 'genteel tradition.'

It is well to remember that these anti-traditionalists have themselves behind them a considerable tradition. Their notion of creativeness has come down essentially unmodified from the eighteenth century; it is an outgrowth of the primitivistic opposition established about that time between the 'natural' and the 'artificial.' As a result of this opposition there was a growing prepossession in favor of the uncultivated epoch and the uncultivated individual. To be accounted an original genius one must, according to the more advanced primitivist, be positively hirsute. 'Poetry,' as Diderot put it, 'calls for something enormous, barbaric and savage.' To be cultivated is to be imitative; whereas, if one is to create, one must be imaginatively and emotionally spontaneous. From this repudiation of imitation in favor of spontaneity have flowed innumerable consequences down to the present day, not merely in art and literature but in life.

The originality of the creator was conceived almost from the start, not only as spontaneous, but as something over which he has little control. 'An original,' we read in Edward Young (1759), 'may be said to be of a vegetable nature.... It grows, it is not made.' For 'vegetable' Coleridge, in the wake of the Germans, substituted 'organic' — still an epithet to conjure with. Here is the point of departure for the distinction between genius and mere talent of which the early romantics made so much. According to Hazlitt 'talent is a voluntary power, while genius is involuntary.' In short the man who knows what he is about is not a genius. The contrast between the organic and spontaneous and the merely imitative and mechanical is closely connected with the predominant interest in the unconscious, as compared with the conscious, which has assumed so many forms from the eighteenth century down to the psycho-analysts. Carlyle makes of the unconscious the source not merely of creative genius but of religious wisdom. 'The difference between Socrates and

[4]

Jesus Christ!' he exclaims. 'The Great Conscious!
The immeasurably greater Unconscious! The one
cunningly manufactured; the other created, living
and life-giving,' et cetera.

The association of creation with spontaneity involved not merely an emancipation of the instincts
and emotions but also, as I have just remarked,
of the imagination. The emergence of the phrase
'creative imagination' marks a decisive step in the
break with neo-classicism. The creativeness of the
imagination is measured, as anyone who has been
through the 'genius' books of the eighteenth century will testify, not by its truth to the universal,
but by its attainment of novelty. A boundless intoxication with novelty is indeed the outstanding
trait of the modern era that sets it off from all the
ages of the past. In literature and the arts this has
meant an almost exclusive emphasis on invention.
A major factor in the discrediting of the principle of
imitation in favor of invention has no doubt been
the prodigious achievements of physical science.
The artists and men of letters have sought to vie
in wonderfulness with their scientific brethren.
Their inventions and novelties have not, however,

met the test of reality like the discoveries of science. They have been to a great extent the result of allowing one's imagination to expatiate at large in some 'empire of chimeras' or else of a striving to express the ineffable something wherein one differs from other men — what Mr. Brownell terms one's uniquity. It may be said indeed that, as a consequence of over a century of the indulgence of idiosyncrasy, the cup of our uniquity is full to overflowing. An idea of creation, one-sided from the start, has finally led in its extreme forms to a veritable cult of the subrational and the abnormal. In all its forms it reflects our modern drift towards naturalism. The very epithet 'creative' was once reserved for what is above nature — as, for example, in the old Latin hymn *Veni Creator Spiritus*. The growth of the naturalistic temper may be measured by the gap between this use of the epithet and the use of it that appears in such phrases as 'creative chemistry' and 'creative salesmanship.'

I

If we really wish to clarify this whole subject of creation we need to go farther back than the modern or even than the medieval period to the sources of occidental thinking in Plato and Aristotle. Plato is more responsible than any other one person for a notion that has enjoyed great popularity down the centuries — the notion that the poet if he is to be truly creative must be 'furious' or 'mad.' In the somewhat enigmatical dialogue *Ion*, the notion assumes a form that reminds one, at least superficially, of the primitivistic cult of the unconscious and the spontaneous. 'Whilst a man retains any portion of the thing called reason,' says the Platonic Socrates, 'he is utterly incompetent to produce poetry.' *Ion* has as a rule been taken to be highly flattering to the poet; but, assuming that the dialogue is by Plato at all, one is inclined to suspect in it an elaborate irony designed to show the inferiority of the poet to the Socratic dialectician. The obvious comment on the opposition Plato sets up between creation and general culture is that it simply does not correspond to the facts of great poetry, so far as we know them. In the case of at least one great poet, Dante, we are not left to conjecture. 'Let the folly of those persons be confessed,' he writes, 'who, lacking art and knowledge and trusting their genius alone, rush forward to sing of the highest themes in the highest way; let them desist from such great folly and, if they are geese by their native sloth, let them not seek to imitate the star-questing eagle.' The Platonic theory of poetic inspiration has served only too often to encourage the conceit of minor poets; it also led to the grotesque attempts of certain pseudo-classic critics to retain poetic fury and at the same time subject it to rules. Father Mambrun, for example, says that the writer of an epic should not be furious in framing his plot, but may sprinkle in a little poetic fury in his episodes.

Moreover, the question may be raised whether all those who invoke Plato are to be accounted his true followers. One of the most recent critics to proclaim that the poet should be 'mad' is Mr. J. E. Spingarn. Is the madness that he praises really of the Platonic type? If we are to do justice to Plato's theory of inspiration we must interpret it in the total spirit of his writings. When thus interpreted, it will be found to look forward to the Christian doctrine of divine grace; whereas the spontaneity of the primitivist is a sort of subrational parody of this doctrine, a substitution, as one may say, for the grace of God of the grace of Nature. When Mr. Spingarn urges us in the name of creation to get rid of both inner and outer inhibitions and let ourselves go,[1] it would seem fairly evident that he is primitivistic rather than Platonic. Only an extreme primitivist, one might suppose, could affirm, as he did some years ago, that 'the art of a child is art quite as much as that of Michelangelo.'[2]

The whole subject is to be sure extremely elusive. It is especially fitting in dealing with the creative process to recall the old saying: 'All things end in a mystery.' One encounters here even more promptly than elsewhere a something indefinable — what the French of the seventeenth century were wont to call a *je ne sais quoi*. Divine grace itself is, according to Father Bouhours, a *je ne sais quoi*. One may, however, discriminate practically and concretely between things, which, in their ultimate essence, elude us and must ever elude us. The problem of poetic 'madness' is very much bound up with that of enthusiasm. There is a superrational enthusiasm that one may properly associate with Plato at his best.

[1] See *Creative Criticism*, p. 120.
[2] *Journal of Philosophy*, vol. 11, no. 12, p. 327.

ON BEING CREATIVE

This quality of enthusiasm, as it manifests itself in the great poets and religious seers, has been defined as 'exalted peace.' It is important to distinguish between the Platonic enthusiasm and that of the primitivist, if one is to deal adequately with the problem of creation. At bottom the primitivist recognizes only one form of enthusiasm, his own. The opposition he established in the eighteenth century between the original genius, on the one hand, and, on the other, the formalist and dry rationalist is still current. One of the most popular forms of this opposition is found in Nietzsche's *Birth of Tragedy*. Dionysos, as there presented, stands for the creative urge, Apollo for a merely formalistic art and Socrates for an uninspired and disintegrating rationalism.[1] But there is also an Apollonian enthusiasm, even worthier of the name, on strictly etymological grounds, than the Dionysiac intoxication, which, as Nietzsche understands it, is plainly

---

[1] One should add that the 'form' that Nietzsche associates with Apollo reminds one in certain respects less of pseudo-classic 'form' than of 'form' as conceived by Schiller in his *Æsthetic Letters* and his poem *The Realm of Shadows*. To Apollo are due 'clarity and precision,' but clarity and precision in a world of pure appearance; reality abides with Dionysos representing the push of 'the primordial One.'

emotional: inasmuch as exalted peace would seem to be more 'divine' than mere emotion, however vehement. Perhaps there is nothing higher in man than the spirit that shapes and controls and sets bounds to lawless expansion. In art and literature this spirit is felt, in contrast with technique or outer form, as inner form or 'soul,' if one may venture to employ a word that has been almost hopelessly cheapened by the emotionalists.

II

If it is important in dealing with our notion of creativeness to distinguish between a true and a false Platonism it is even more important to deal adequately with the doctrine of imitation; for the whole modern movement can be shown to be rooted in a revolt from this doctrine. For a sound doctrine of imitation we need to turn from Plato to Aristotle. Plato conceived of imitation in the arts as something literal and uninspired and therefore so disparaged it as to prepare the way for later obscurantists; whereas Aristotle bends his whole effort to showing that imitation may be ideal, or, as we should say, creative. It becomes creative in direct proportion as it succeeds in rendering the universal through the particular. Poetry that has been thus successful has *spoudaiotes*, the term that Matthew Arnold (probably following Goethe) has rendered 'high seriousness.' Chapter IX of the *Poetics*, in which Aristotle insists on the representative and highly serious quality of great poetry, disposes once for all of Mrs. Colum's contention that the treatise is written from the point of view of the tired business man. Yet Mrs. Colum is right in a sense in thinking that if Aristotle's *Poetics* were discredited the whole structure of classicism would collapse at the base; not that classicism rests on the authority of Aristotle or any other authority as such, but that it does require in some form or other a doctrine of the universal and that the *Poetics* contains the earliest and still, on the whole, the most satisfactory account of the process of creative imitation by which the artist may hope to achieve the universal.

Aristotle's *katharsis*, the most discussed term in criticism, can be interpreted rightly only in the light of his doctrine of the universal. A great tragedy portrays passion and portrays it vividly; at the same time it generalizes it. The spectator who is thus lifted into the atmosphere of the universal tends to be purged of everything that is petty and purely personal in his own emotions. He partakes in some measure of the exalted peace that is felt in the back-ground of true tragedy. He is 'dismissed,' in Milton's phrase, with 'calm of mind all passion spent.' One should note in passing that the treatise *On the Sublime* attributed to Longinus, which contrasts sharply by its genuinely Platonic temper with the dryly analytical *Poetics*, yet agrees with it in an essential particular: the Longinian sublimity or elevation requires, like the Aristotelian high seriousness, truth to the universal.

Finally, if one is to grasp Aristotle's full meaning, one needs to connect what he says about the universal not only with what he says about *katharsis* but also with what he says about 'myth' or fiction. The poet who seeks to be representative must, like Homer, know how to tell lies skilfully. He must, in short, be a master of illusion, but the illusion should, as Goethe puts it, be that of a higher reality. The advantage of this whole conception is that it is not

[13]

theoretical: it simply states the effect actually produced upon one by artistic and literary creation of the first order.

The neo-classics, in taking over from Aristotle the idea of probability or truth to the universal, tended to eliminate from it the element of illusion or, as we should say, the imaginative element. Moreover, they hoped to achieve their universal not so much by the direct imitation of 'nature' (in the Aristotelian sense, human nature in purposeful action) as by the imitation of models, of those writers whose reputations were consecrated by a constant and general admiration (the Longinian test of literary excellence), and who were therefore presumed to be a sort of 'second nature.' The imitation of models, it is well to remember, is not necessarily barren. Many of the neo-classics showed that this type of imitation is compatible with genuine creation. Pope, for example, is genuinely creative in his imitation of Horace's Epistle to Augustus. The imitation of models is legitimate, as Joubert says, provided that it be the imitation of one spirit by another spirit and not of one book by another book. The imitation of many of the minor neo-classics was, it

[14]

must be admitted, of this latter kind and so degenerated into mere copyism.

The primitivists had at least this excuse in rejecting the whole principle of imitation as a pseudo-classic convention, and in beginning their long warfare on culture in the name of creative spontaneity. The evident drawback of linking creativeness with spontaneity rather than with imitation is that it leads to a loss of the representative quality. The moderns, whether impressionists or expressionists, romantics or realists, would seem to have achieved to a lesser degree than the creators of certain epochs of the past, the 'grandeur of generality.' The drift towards eccentricity has also been encouraged by the purely exploratory attitude towards life of physical science — an attitude that when carried over into the realm of human values may easily degenerate into pseudo-science. Taine, for example, is pseudo-scientific when he declares that 'sleep, madness, delirium, somnambulism, hallucination, offer a much more profitable field of experiment for the psychology of the individual than the normal state.' As the result of a one-sided devotion to the divergent and the exceptional on the part of various brands of naturalists, we have become incapable, according to M. Léon Séché, of creating general types. 'The abnormal, the monstrous, the improbable alone attract our attention.' It is well not to make such statements too sweepingly of one's contemporaries; yet the danger surely lies in the direction M. Séché has indicated. Jules Lemaître complained of the eccentrics of his day that they were turning literature into a 'mysterious diversion of mandarins.' The diversion has become even more mysterious since. Certain *surréalistes* have indeed proclaimed in the name of creation, conceived as pure self-expression, that the writer is under no obligation to communicate to the reader anything at all.

The same disparagement of communication in the interests of self-expression has been visible in the other arts — notably in painting. One may illustrate this point apropos of the remarkable assertion of Miss Rebecca West that Cézanne is the 'heir of Poussin.' [1] One may grant that there are peripheral overlappings between the two painters (Cézanne had a genuine admiration for Poussin), but these over-

[1] *Bookman*, August, 1930, p. 517.

lappings should not obscure the central divergence. All is not mere formalism in the neo-classic view, accepted by Poussin, that the painter should not depict ordinary nature but a selected and ennobled nature (*la belle nature*). Something of this finer symmetry and more perfect proportion he actually succeeds in conveying in his landscapes. This creative selection is not to be confounded with the creative distortion one finds in Cézanne and his followers, a distortion that, like so much else in modern art, has its source in an eagerness for lyrical self-expression.[1] In its extreme manifestations this eagerness has led to a denial that painting need concern itself with representation. Some of the modernist painters have gone even farther than the early German romantics who, in their desire to emancipate the creative imagination, proclaimed that the highest form of art is the arabesque.

One should note the transformation that has taken place in certain critical terms as a result of the divorce of the idea of creation from that of the

---

[1] For the relationship between the theory and practice of Cézanne and the expressionistic exaggerations of certain recent painters see *Modern Painting* by F. J. Mather, p. 334 ff.

universal. *Katharsis* has been appropriated by the psycho-analysts to describe the relief one gets by expressing oneself freely. The idea itself is at least as old as the romantic movement. Poetry, says Byron, 'is the lava of the imagination whose eruption prevents the earthquake.' The epithet sublime has also ceased to be associated with the universal. Elevation, which is primary in the Longinian definition of the term, has tended to give way to sheer emotional intensity. Rousseau, for example, says that he was 'sublime' in the eloquence he displayed in his philanderings with Madame d'Houdetot. The modernist movement abounds in persons who, like Mr. Spingarn, are for getting rid, at least in art, of both outer and inner inhibitions and letting themselves go and who, at the same time, set up as sublime 'idealists.'

Idealism of this sort leads inevitably to an era of 'debunking.' Unfortunately debunkers of the type of Mr. H. L. Mencken are part of the very disease they are attacking. They have got rid of the false sublime but not of the false *katharsis*. 'The critic,' says Mr. Mencken, 'is first and last simply trying to express himself.... He is trying to achieve thereby

for his own inner ego the grateful feeling of a function performed, a tension relieved, a *katharsis* attained which Wagner achieved when he wrote *Die
Walküre* and a hen achieves every time she lays an
egg.' What Mr. Mencken understands by self-expression he has told us elsewhere: 'An author like
any other so-called artist is a man in whom the
normal vanity of all men is so vastly exaggerated
that he finds it a sheer impossibility to hold it in.
His overpowering impulse is to gyrate before his
fellow-men, flapping his wings and emitting defiant
yells. This being forbidden by the *polizei* of all
civilized countries, he takes it out by putting his
yells on paper. Such is the thing called self-expression.' Here, one must admit, is the ultimate worm's-
eye view of both *katharsis* and self-expression. It is
Mr. Mencken's special gift, indeed, to attain the
ultimate worm's-eye view of most of the topics on
which he touches. As a result of his efforts and those
of his kind we have been getting rid not only of the
false sublime but also of the true. We seem to be
losing the very idea of nobility and elevation.[1]

[1] See the essay *Farewell to Achilles* by Alan Reynolds Thompson
(*The Bookman*, January, 1930).

ON BEING CREATIVE

III

It has been urged that the standard of high seriousness and truth to the universal has always been impracticably high and has tended to blind those who have accepted it to the merits of much genuinely creative art and literature both past and present. The late Stuart Sherman accused me in particular of erecting a '*chevaux-de-frise* of arbitrary definition warranted to eviscerate every gizzard and break every neck born into this disastrous world since Aristotle.' It is only fair to Sherman to add that he made this absurd statement in a moment of irritation and in a private letter. If publishers confined themselves to printing 'highly serious' books, either new or old, most of them would be bankrupt in a very few months. No sensible person would maintain that the creative imitation expounded by Aristotle exhausts the idea of creation. Books may minister to utility or recreation or wisdom. To books in all three classes the epithet 'creative' may in some sense or other be applied. One cannot discriminate between one class and another simply by an appeal to the principle of pleasure. Aristotle says that tragedy should give its own appropriate pleasure; but then a cook-book may also give its appropriate pleasure. The two pleasures are, however, of a very different order. If Aristotle were living today, it is conceivable that he might in his recreative moments find solace in a good detective story. What is not conceivable is that he would put fiction of this quality on a level with the representative fiction he has described in his *Poetics*. One should add that work that belongs in the recreative class may transcend infinitely in merit detective stories and the like. Some of the best of the world's poetry has been less concerned with a deeper interpretation of the facts of life than with an escape from them. Keats's *Ode to a Nightingale* is an especially exquisite poem of escape.

The great problem is to avoid a confusion of categories. Humanist and anti-humanist have each accused the other of a confusion of this kind. If the humanist makes a plea for the literature of wisdom he is told by the anti-humanist that he speaks not as a literary critic but as a philosopher. The literary critic does not allow alien ethical considerations to intrude into the realm of art, holding as he does that beauty is its own excuse for being. High seriousness, according to President Neilson of Smith, is something that may be left to divines; the poet should be satisfied if he attains intensity. The point of view is related to a notion that dates from the dawn of the modernist movement — namely, that there is no intermediary term between mere moralism and æsthetic irresponsibility. Creative work, in order to be accounted highly serious, does not need to aim primarily at edification, as certain neo-classic critics were too prone to suppose; it does need to have centrality of vision or, if one prefers, to be informed by an imagination that is disciplined to some truly human norm. Such a criterion may seem difficult and elusive, but it is the only one that is finally valid.

Let us turn to the confusion of categories with which the humanist charges his modernist opponent. Here again everything hinges on the quality of imagination displayed by the creator. Numerous persons whose imaginations were really 'wandering wild' in some 'empire of chimeras' have during the past century set up as philosophic teachers and even as religious seers, and been received as such by critics and public. For instance, Professor C. H. Herford asserts that Shelley has in *Prometheus Un-*

bound given 'magnificent expression to the faith of Plato and of Christ.' The confusion revealed by such an utterance is far graver than that of the neo-classic who thought he was highly serious when he was in fact only didactic.

The person who wishes to avoid primitivistic and other confusions needs to be keenly critical. Anyone who is thus critical will protest first of all against the sharp line that is now drawn between critics and creators with a view to disparaging the former. Our writers have fallen into a veritable cant on the subject of creation. The ordinary distinction between creative and critical writing is to be sure convenient and indeed inevitable. At the same time one should remember that an even more fundamental distinction than that between criticism and creation is that between good and bad literature. Good literature may be defined as literature which combines excellence of form with soundness of substance. Much writing that is usually classified as critical will be found to satisfy this definition. A great critic is a rare apparition — even rarer, according to Tennyson, than a great poet. One should not therefore deny the element of truth in the notion that there is a hierarchy of genres. A great poet, especially a great dramatic poet, deserves to outrank even a great critic. What is absurd is to disparage a good critic as compared with some inferior poet or novelist on the ground that he is less creative. One should beware of the same error in dealing with the different works of one author. Is Dryden less creative in his *Essay of Dramatic Poesy* than in *Aurengzebe*, or Johnson less creative in the *Lives of the Poets* than in *Irene*, or Sainte-Beuve less creative in the *Lundis* than in *Volupté*? In that case so much the worse for creation.

According to Miss Rebecca West, the superiority of Aristotle to Rousseau is so generally recognized that anyone who asserts it will have the air of 'exhibiting as a rare jewel' something that is really 'about as rare as a nickel.' [1] Now Rousseau probably did more than anyone else to associate creation with the uttering of one's uniqueness and so to usher in the age of genius. Miss West makes clear her own affiliations when she repudiates the members of the humanistic group as creatively impotent in comparison with the ultra-modernists. Mr. More, one

[1] *The Bookman*, August, 1930, p. 516.

is led to infer, is less creative in the five volumes of
The Greek Tradition (which Miss West seems nevertheless to admire) than, let us say, Mr. James Joyce
in his *Work in Progress*. It is only too plain that
Miss West herself must be numbered among those
whom Mr. More has termed 'the victims of genius.'
The Rousseauistic fallacies that have ensnared so
clever a person cannot be dismissed as merely trite
and obvious.

IV

There is a sense in which the critic may aspire to
be creative but one needs to define with extreme
care what this sense is. The creative critic, as cur-
rently conceived, is only a variant of the original
genius. The impression he receives from the creative
expression of another is so vivid and so colored
by his temperamental uniqueness that, when re-
expressed, it deserves, he holds, to count as a fresh
creation. Creative criticism in this sense is in germ
in the tendency of the older romantics to set up
gusto as a substitute for taste. Critics like Hazlitt
and Lamb display a keenness of literary relish that
is often not only delectable in itself but legitimate,

[25]

though even in Hazlitt and Lamb the relish prevails unduly at times over judgment. One's enjoyment of Lamb's essay on *The Artificial Comedy of the Last Century*, for example, needs to be tempered by the reflection that it has little relation to the facts. A pleasant paradox like Lamb's is occasionally justified by way of protest against an unduly smug acquiescence in the orthodox view. If, however, one follows the trend down to Oscar Wilde (*The Critic as Artist*) one finds a creativeness that is plainly anarchical, a creativeness that relieves the critic of allegiance to anything that might serve as a check on the wanderings of his imagination and sensibility.

It is possible to attach an entirely different meaning to the epithet creative as applied to the critic. There is need of a type of critic who will essay the task, especially difficult under existing circumstances, of creating standards. Without standards there can be no center of judgment to which to refer the mere welter of appearances. Lacking this center, other forms of creation will become unstructural and so sink to a comparatively low level. As a result of the failure to achieve thus far any such coördinating principle of unity, the whole modern experiment is in danger of assuming the aspect of a return to chaos.

The coördinating principle has as a rule been supplied by tradition. A striking trait of the modernist on the other hand, as should be sufficiently clear from all I have said, is that he is not merely untraditional but anti-traditional in his notions of creation. He hopes in his own phrase to base his originality on 'certain enormous repudiations.' The true modern, in contradistinction to the modernist, holds that tradition is indispensable. It does not mean for him, however, a return to dogma but rather a completion and enrichment of present experience by that of the past. In casting about for a concrete example of someone who has combined a modern outlook on life with a right attitude towards tradition one thinks almost inevitably of Goethe. The Goethe who is revealed, for example, in the *Conversations* with Eckermann is fairly free from the fallacies of the age of genius (including a number in which he had himself indulged). Anyone who is seeking a reintegration of judgment in criticism and an escape from the present impressionistic-expressionistic imbroglio can scarcely afford to neglect him.

The person, however, who wishes to array

ON BEING CREATIVE

Goethe on the side of judgment has to explain the curious circumstance that, as interpreted by Mr. Spingarn, he has been one of the sponsors for the highly modernistic theory of criticism and creation that has prevailed in this country of late years. According to Goethe, as cited by Spingarn,[1] the critic should ask himself the following questions: 'What has the writer proposed to himself to do? and how far has he succeeded in carrying out his own plan?' A man is said once to have succeeded in carving images of the twelve apostles on a single cherry stone. A living German is reported to have constructed a perfect model of Cologne Cathedral out of two million and a half match sticks. The critic is apparently to be confined to congratulating such persons or those who undertake the literary equivalent on their success in accomplishing what they set out to do. But before attributing any such absurdity to Goethe let us verify Mr. Spingarn's quotation. We then discover that Goethe would have the critic ask a third question: 'Was the author's plan reasonable and sensible?'[2] Mr. Spingarn owes the public

[1] *Creative Criticism*, p. 20.
[2] See Goethe's review of Manzoni's *Conte di Carmagnola* (*Jubi-*

[28]

ON BEING CREATIVE

an explanation of how he came to reduce Goethe's three questions to two, with the result of transforming him from an Aristotelian humanist into a Crocean æsthete.

Goethe seems indeed in certain of his utterances to give a very subordinate place to the judicial element in criticism. One needs to remember in regard to such utterances that there is in criticism as elsewhere a truth and a counter-truth. The truth is that the critic worthy of the name must judge; the counter-truth is that he should base his judgment on the widest comprehension and sympathy. The humanistic critic does not cultivate exclusively either the truth or the counter-truth but mediates between them; only, according to the special conditions with which he has to deal, he may lean to one side or the other. Goethe leaned very strongly to the side of comprehension and sympathy as a corrective to the dogmatic narrowness of many of the critics of his time.

läums Ausgabe, vol. 37, pp. 179–90). As a matter of fact Goethe has lifted the three questions bodily from the first paragraph of Manzoni's preface to this work. The portion of the review containing the questions appears correctly in Goethe's Literary Essays: A Selection in English arranged by J. E. Spingarn (p. 140). The omission of the third question in Creative Criticism was noted independently by Norman Foerster in his American Criticism (p. 119).

ON BEING CREATIVE

The present emergency is the exact opposite of the one that confronted Goethe. Open-mindedness is being glorified in the critic as an end in itself. As a matter of fact critics who were developing breadth but were in the process losing standards were beginning to appear even in Goethe's day. Thus A. W. Schlegel had extended his comprehension and sympathy over a wide area of art and literature, much of it intrinsically worth while, that had been either neglected or disparaged by the neo-classic critics. He could not, however, be trusted to apply to his immense acquisition a correct scale of values. 'I look upon his treatment of the French drama,' said Goethe, 'as a sort of recipe for the formation of a bad critic.' There could be no doubt, Goethe admitted, as to his great learning; but then, he added, 'All the learning in the world is still no judgment.'

This latter remark is especially relevant to our contemporary world except that its breadth of knowledge does not as a rule inhere in the individual but has been divided up among a multitude of specialists. Anyone who sets out nowadays to create standards with a view to the rehabilitation of judgment will find that he will need to make a frontal at-

tack on the doctrine of spontaneity, not indeed as incompatible with certain forms of creation, legitimate
enough in their own place and degree, but as the
basis for an adequate philosophy of life. The confusion of categories that results from the attempt to
give to spontaneity a supreme and central place I
have already indicated. Emerson imports this confusion into ethics when he avers in one of his more
Rousseauistic moments that 'our moral nature is
vitiated by any interference of our will.' Fichte
extends the idea of ethical spontaneity to the whole
body of Teutons. They have character, he says,
without conscious effort on their part, being as they
are an *Urvolk*, the elect of nature. The danger of
thus encouraging mere expansiveness, whether in an
individual or in a people, should by this time be
manifest. The stormy emancipation that began in
Goethe's youth, not merely from the traditional
controls but from any limitations whatsoever, may
perhaps be symbolized in the figure of Faust. According to Spengler, the Faustian man is now dying.
It is high time he should die if civilization is to live
— true civilization and not civilization in the very
special sense that Spengler himself gives to the term.

ON BEING CREATIVE

Standards not only set limits to mere expansiveness but will be found to imply, so far as the temperamental man is concerned, the setting up of a model of some sort, in other words a revival of the principle of imitation. One may admit the possibility that some individual may, single-handed, achieve a sound synthesis and at the same time give it creative embodiment, let us say, in poetry. If we are to go by the experience of the past, however, we must conclude that important religious or humanistic art and literature require normally the support of a convention. If as a result of a vigorous critical movement a considerable number of persons not only got together as to the essentials of the good life, but insisted on making their agreement effective in education, they might be preparing the way for a very different type of creation from the two main types that have flourished for several generations past — the romantic and the so-called realistic. It has been proclaimed on various occasions in this country that it is time for us to give over following old-world patterns and to express our native genius. But the very notion of genius implied in this programme is itself a dubious borrowing from the old world. If we were

really capable of virile initiative we should be bringing a searching scrutiny to bear on this whole notion
of genius and its outcome in art and literature from
the eighteenth century down. It is not likely that
we should then be content, as we have been for the
most part of recent years, to echo belatedly a decadent European naturalism.

II

THE PRIMITIVISM OF
WORDSWORTH

DIFFERENT ages have different ways of being
pedantic or, if one prefers, of losing their sense of
proportion. A favorite way in our own age is to
attach an exaggerated importance to the merely
historical and biographical element in literary criticism. What should at most be the frame of the
picture has tended, as someone has put it, to take
the place of the picture itself. The critic offers as
a substitute for an estimate of an author's work
minute inquiry into his life; at his worst he sinks
to the level of gossip — often malignant gossip.

This unbalanced type of criticism has been
especially evident in recent studies of the romantic
movement and can indeed be shown to derive
largely from it. The more important of these
studies have been listed, along with the older
material, by Dr. Ernest Bernbaum in his *Guide
Through the Romantic Movement*, the first volume of

his useful five-volume anthology of the English romantics and pre-romantics. The question forces itself upon one whether Dr. Bernbaum's own critical judgment has kept pace with his historical scholarship when he asserts that the study of the romantic movement 'should be the most illuminating literary discipline the world has ever known.' As appears from the context, he has been led to make this singular statement by the fact that it is possible to immerse one's self more completely in historical and biographical detail in dealing with the romantics than it is with the writers of the remoter literary epochs.

The investigators have been especially busy of late with Wordsworth and his background in the eighteenth century, with results that are often of interest in their proper subordinate place. New light has been thrown on Wordsworth's own development by Professor de Selincourt's volume containing hitherto unpublished versions of the *Prelude* (especially the redaction of 1805) along with the text that finally appeared in 1850. The modifications Wordsworth introduced into the successive versions frequently reflect the changes in his outlook

[35]

on life from his youthful radicalism to the Anglican orthodoxy of his old age.

An especially choice morsel for the ultra-biographically inclined, it is scarcely necessary to say, has been the unearthing by Professors Harper and Legouis of the facts concerning Wordsworth's liaison with Annette Vallon during his early residence in France (1792). Professor Legouis, indeed, appears to have felt at least passing qualms [1] at having allied himself with what one is tempted to call the Paul Pry school of criticism. His enjoyment of one of the best sonnets in English ('It is a beauteous Evening, calm and free') seems to have been impaired by his knowledge of the fact that Wordsworth meant it, not for his sister Dorothy, as had hitherto been supposed, but for his natural daughter Caroline. 'The sonnet offers,' he says, 'a striking example of the way in which Wordsworth was wont to solemnize the most profane passages of his life.... There is indeed a wonderful forgetfulness of contingencies, a rare lack of self-compunction in the father, a fragile sinner, who transforms himself into a sovereign pontiff.'

[1] See his *Wordsworth in a New Light*, p. 42.

THE PRIMITIVISM OF WORDSWORTH

In the meanwhile, if we are to judge by the two most recent volumes on Wordsworth, one by Herbert Read and the other by the late Professor C. H. Herford, there has been along with all this bustle of research into his life retrogression rather than advance in the critical estimate of his poetry. Both books are written with distinction and contain much that is acceptable in detail. The contrast in point of view is not only that between two individuals, but between two generations. Mr. Herford is an unusually complacent humanitarian of a familiar nineteenth-century type. He not only exalts a kindred 'idealism' in Wordsworth during what he terms the 'golden years,' but also the type of nationalism that appears in the tract on *The Convention of Cintra*. Mr. Read, on the contrary, is inclined to regard Wordsworth in this tract as the 'prophet of a polity that reached its natural conclusion in the world war of 1914–1918.' In general Mr. Read does not take Wordsworth's philosophy seriously. He is more interested in tracing the 'tortuous development of his mind through the ten years that elapsed between his passion for Annette Vallon, and his marriage with Mary

THE PRIMITIVISM OF WORDSWORTH

Hutchinson.' The drift away from critical evaluation towards biographical irrelevancies has received a fresh impetus in his case from his acceptance of psycho-analysis. This means practically that he tends to interpret even what seems most impersonal in Wordsworth's poetry in terms of Annette Vallon. For example, if Wordsworth lost faith in France it was 'because he was transferring to this symbol France the effects of his cooling affection for Annette.' Mr. Read does not pause to consider that during the last decade of the eighteenth century numerous other radicals with no Annettes in their background suffered precisely the same loss of faith in France when it ceased to be the 'champion of human kind' and grew imperialistic. One should add that Mr. Read does not think any the less highly of Wordsworth because in his own phrase 'the greatness of his poetry is grounded in animal passions.' On the contrary, the quality of this poetry seems to him 'not much lower than Shakespeare's.'

The appropriate comment on Mr. Read's attempt to dispose of Wordsworth psycho-analytically would seem to be the celebrated one of Jeffrey:

THE PRIMITIVISM OF WORDSWORTH

'This will never do.' Without disdaining any subsidiary aid that may be derived from biography, one
must agree on the whole with Wordsworth when he
declares that poetical works 'contain within themselves all that is necessary to their being compre-
hended and relished,' and, one may add, judged.
Few poets have ever striven harder than Wordsworth to be philosophical. In itself his ambition
to write verse that was not only delightful but
wise was perfectly legitimate. One's opinion as to
the measure of his success will depend on what
one thinks of the philosophy he held during his
most creative years (approximately 1797 to 1807),
a philosophy which may be defined as primitivism.

I

Before coming to this philosophy in Wordsworth
himself, it may be well to review rapidly the
eighteenth-century preparation for primitivism. It
is not without interest to trace the origins of a
movement that is in itself a glorification of origins.
This movement was in its essential aspect a reaction
from the two great traditions of the Occident — the

classical and the Christian. These two traditions were, it must be confessed, in certain respects vulnerable, not to speak of the fact that they were not in entire accord with one another. The classical tradition had come to suffer, especially in connection with its central doctrine of decorum, from a taint of formalism. Those who sought to escape from this formalism set up a cult of original genius and creative imagination of which I have spoken elsewhere in this volume. The Christian tradition, again, with its central emphasis on man's fallen state and the consequent need of humility, had been developed by Calvin and others into a theological nightmare. Pascal, for example, had said that man is an insoluble enigma to himself without the dogma of infant damnation. 'The corruption of the heart of man,' said Jonathan Edwards, 'is a thing that is immoderate and boundless in its fury.'

Rousseau's discovery that man is naturally good is to be understood largely as an extreme recoil from the theological nightmare. Wordsworth writes in *The Prelude:*

> I had approached, like other youths, the shield
> Of human nature from the golden side,

THE PRIMITIVISM OF WORDSWORTH

> And would have fought even to the death to attest
> The quality of the metal which I saw.

This eagerness to attest the quality of the human metal is even more Rousseauistic than youthful. One needs to remember, however, that there were many English anticipations of Rousseau's ideas. Much in Wordsworth that reminds one of Rousseau derives rather from these English sources. There is a side of the third Earl of Shaftesbury that is especially influential in the later eighteenth century not only in England but in other countries — the side that may be summed up in such phrases as moral æstheticism and incipient sentimentalism. Shaftesbury is growing emotional not only in his conception of conscience, but in his attitude towards the revelation of the divine that he saw in the forms of outer nature. He attacks the older type of religious enthusiasm — the type that appears in the partisans of the 'inner light' in the seventeenth century. At the same time he prepares the way for the new romantic enthusiasm. One can follow, for example, the religious response to the landscape that appears in his Rhapsody to Nature, through poets like Akenside, Thomson, and others, until finally sentimental deism passes by almost insensible stages into the emotional pantheism of *Tintern Abbey*.

The essential idea that one needs to trace in the rehabilitation of both man and nature that was taking place in the eighteenth century is that of sympathy. Some of the founders of the new morality looked on sympathy as innate, others derived it from the principle of association. One of the associationists, David Hartley, is supposed to have had so much influence on Wordsworth that a whole book [1] has been largely devoted to the subject.

Those who were thus encouraging a release of the emotions were reacting not only from neo-classic formalism and an unduly austere theology, but also from certain very unflattering views of human nature that were more or less outside of the two great traditions. Not to speak of the misanthropic Swift, whose case is a somewhat special one, there was the cynical Mandeville, who by his assertion that the will to power is stronger in the natural man than the benevolent impulses, links up with Hobbes

[1] *William Wordsworth: His Doctrine and Art in Their Historical Relations*, by Arthur Beatty (1922).

and in some respects with Machiavelli, and puts himself squarely in opposition to Shaftesbury. Then there were the survivors of the wicked wits of the Restoration who took it to be the business of the stage

> To hold to every man a faithful glass
> And show him of what species he's an ass.

Some sought like Addison to retain wit, but to purge it of its lewdness and ill-nature — in short to make it respectable at some risk, it must be confessed, of making it dull. What was finally to prevail, however, was not wit, either reformed or unreformed, but sensibility. It is important to remember that the emergence of the man of feeling coincides with the rise of the middle class to power and influence. One can understand that the man of the middle class should have grown weary of being flouted by the wits, as he had been, for example, in the drama of the Restoration. He was well within his rights in insisting that he be taken seriously both on the stage and in real life. What was dubious was the middle-class tendency to estimate a man's innate goodness by his effusiveness and even by his lachrymosity.

[43]

Finally, one should remember that the sentimentalists of the eighteenth century, precursors of the emotional romanticists of the nineteenth, were seeking a solution of the dilemma created by the philosophers. By his denial of a transcendent element in man, Locke in particular seemed to have written over what had been traditionally regarded as the ascending path to wisdom: 'No Thoroughfare.' The rationalism that he and others offered as a substitute was found to be unsatisfying; above all it did not satisfy man's deep-seated craving for immediacy: so that presently he began to turn for this immediacy to the region of impulse and instinct that lies below the rational level. The result was an ever-growing prepossession in favor of the natural as compared with the artificial, of the spontaneous as compared with the imitative. The poet no longer sought his inspiration, like certain religious poets of the past, in the supersensuous, nor again, like the humanistic poets, in society, but in nature and in those whom he regarded as close to nature. He often developed a predilection for periods of the past and those regions of the earth in the present (for example, the islands of the South

Sea) that had not been contaminated by civilization.[1] Imagination became more and more an
imaging of nature, especially in its wilder aspects.
This primitivistic drift finally led to the rise of a
type that has been defined as the youthful dreaming
poet. One embodiment of this type, the Edwin of
Beattie's *Minstrel*, appears to have had marked
influence on Wordsworth. According to his sister
Dorothy there is much of Edwin in the Wordsworth
of *The Prelude*.[2]

II

If we are to understand Wordsworth's attitude
towards nature we not only need to keep in mind
this eighteenth-century background, but also to
remember that he was in certain respects a highly
exceptional child. He was exceptional by the
vividness of the impressions he received from
natural objects ('the mighty world of eye and ear');
he was even more exceptional by his tendency at

[1] Primitivistic trends in eighteenth-century England have been
traced by Professor Chauncey B. Tinker in his volume, *Nature's
Simple Plan* (1922).

[2] The subject has been treated in an unpublished Harvard
doctoral dissertation by Professor Earl A. Aldrich on *James Beattie's Minstrel; its Sources and its Influence on the English Romantic
Poets.*

times to doubt the very reality of these objects. It was no ordinary schoolboy who, as he relates, 'was often unable to think of external things as having external existence.... Many times while going to school have I grasped at a wall or tree to recall myself from this abyss of idealism to reality.' The 'idealism' is of a distinctly Berkeleyan type. Actually he attached an importance to early impressions and the associations that develop from them that allies him rather with Hartley. Both the abnormal vividness of the early impressions and the occasional moods in which he doubted the very reality of the world of sense were at one in fostering in him a capacity that was not possessed in a like degree, one may suppose, by either Hartley or Berkeley, and that is a prime virtue in romantic psychology — the capacity, namely, for wonder. He tells how on one occasion a very 'ordinary sight' — that of a girl walking across a barren moor bearing a pitcher on her head — was suddenly invested, as he gazed upon it, with a 'visionary dreariness.'[1]

On a Wordsworth thus romantically endowed

[1] *The Prelude*, XII, 245 ff.

THE PRIMITIVISM OF WORDSWORTH

there came the influence of the French Revolution. His conversion to the cause of man, as he tells us in *The Prelude*, was due largely to his contacts with Michel Beaupuy at Blois (1792). In the first flush of his enthusiasm he saw everything bathed in a sort of idyllic glamour. The real world 'took on the attraction of a country in romance.' We who are living in the twilight of the humanitarian movement can scarcely conceive how seriously Wordsworth and others received the revolutionary promise of immediate and universal regeneration; nor again the bitterness of their disillusion when it became plain that the 'ideal' and the actual were not to coalesce after all. Some, on the fading of their faith in the new palingenesis or rebirth of mankind in the mass, lived, like the Recluse of *The Excursion*, for ever after disconsolate. Wordsworth, having ceased to believe in the establishment of social justice by collective crusading, adopted for a time the rationalistic individualism of Godwin. There was a moment, he tells us, when having renounced Godwinism in turn,[1] he 'yielded up moral questions in

[1] According to M. Legouis, Wordsworth is already anti-Godwinian in his play *The Borderers*; according to Mr. Garrod, he is still Godwinian. The discovery of the original preface to *The*

despair.' His convalescence from this despair
begins with his settling at Racedown in Dorset with
his sister Dorothy (1795), and his intimacy, after
moving to Alfoxden (1797), with Coleridge. The
rôle of Dorothy in this convalescence is comparatively easy to define. He not only developed under
her tutelage the gift he already possessed for observing lovingly and minutely natural objects ('she
gave me eyes, she gave me ears'), but associated this
observation with 'the still sad music of humanity.'
Dorothy reveals in her *Journals* a delicacy of perception that borders at times on hyperæsthesia. We
are reminded of a passage in one of Shelley's letters
in which he complains that his feelings are awakened
at intervals 'to a state of such unnatural and keen
excitement, that, only to instance the organ of
sight, I find the very blades of grass and the boughs
of distant trees present themselves to me with
microscopic distinctness.'

The intellectual stimulus Wordsworth received
from Coleridge was a needful corrective of the influence of Dorothy, which by itself would have been

Borderers by Mr. de Selincourt seems to have settled the question
in favor of M. Legouis.

somewhat debilitating.[1] His debt to Coleridge is not so easy to define as that to his sister. Perhaps we may best determine the nature of this debt by asking wherein Wordsworth differed after his acquaintance with Coleridge from a pure sensationalist and associationist like Hartley, with whom he undoubtedly had much in common. In the first place, Wordsworth differs from Hartley in his distrust of analysis, and in general of the uninspired understanding. Coleridge shows a similar distrust, though it was probably less marked in 1797 than after his initiation into German metaphysics. The anti-intellectual and anti-scientific trend that one finds in Wordsworth during his primitivistic period may perhaps be explained after all as primarily a revulsion from the Godwinian rationalism. The influence of Coleridge is more visible in Wordsworth's tendency not merely to attach great importance to the impressions of sense, especially to the early impressions, as the final source even of what seems highest in man, but to transcendentalize these impressions. Hartley associated God with nature after the fashion of the eighteenth-century

[1] Cf. Legouis: *The Early Life of William Wordsworth*, p. 315.

deist.[1] There is no evidence, however, that he read ineffable meanings into the primrose. The insight that one may not come at directly may, according to Wordsworth, be mediated through the 'light of sense,' which, at the very moment of its extinction, may reveal as 'with a flash... the invisible world.' [2]

Coleridge was later to accuse Wordsworth of 'mental bombast' — an occasional solemnity of tone not justified by the intrinsic importance of his subject matter. Was he not himself responsible in some measure for this bombast in so far as he had encouraged Wordsworth to read a transcendental significance into his youthful contacts with nature? 'Wisdom and Spirit of the universe!' Wordsworth exclaims in the first book of the *Prelude*. This seems a somewhat ambitious prologue for the description of a skating party on Windermere, even though this description be done in his best manner.

III

Most of the influences on Wordsworth I have been enumerating thus far were at least at one in leading him to turn for his wisdom to simple sights

[1] Cf. especially *Observations on Man*, II, Prop. 57.
[2] *Prelude*, VI, vv. 660–02.

and simple people. What it means thus to look for one's illumination backwards and downwards instead of forwards and up has been excellently put by M. Legouis:

Forth step the ignorant and illiterate, whose senses, not yet distorted by analysis, yield them immediate perception of the world...; above all, children, still half enveloped in the mystery which is the origin of every creature.... But the train of those restored to honour is not yet ended. There follow those in whom all purely intellectual light appears extinct — the crazy and the idiotic, to whom the common people, perhaps not wrongly, attribute inspiration, and from whom even the wise may learn much, for none can say beforehand what phrase will issue from their lips; and since the utter impotence of so-called rational beings is admitted, may it not be that these will presently let fall words not less profound than mysterious? And though human beings have now passed by, the procession still continues. Shall the multitudes which the philosophy of a Descartes would proscribe, the animals which cannot reason, be set aside on account of so insignificant a deficiency? They possess the principle of life; they possess instinct.... Nor is even this enough. Plants also have their joys and sorrows; they live and feel; they speak a language which the poet should strive to understand and to interpret.

Wordsworth's primitivism, one needs to recollect, is not only a reaction from the excess of abstract and analytical reasoning that had been encouraged during the period of European culture known as the Enlightenment, but also from neo-classic decorum and imitation. Neo-classic decorum was a far-reaching principle that the poet had to observe in all things, from his choice of words to his choice of subject if he was to attain elegance and nobility. The conventional elegance he thus sought to achieve — I am of course stating neo-classic practice at its worst — he applied to his work from without as a sort of pigment or veneer. To change the metaphor, the relation of language to poetry was conceived to be mechanical, like that of a garment to a body, rather than vital, like that of a body to an informing soul. The result was the 'gaudiness and inane phraseology' which Wordsworth laments. His remedy for this artificiality is primitivistic to the last degree. Instead of being conventionally elegant and imitative, poetry is in his own phrase to be 'the spontaneous overflow of powerful feelings.' This emotional spontaneity is to be found in those who are nearest to nature in the primitivistic sense, so that we must look for the true language of poetry not, like the neo-classicist, to the top but to the bottom of society; to the peasantry, in short, especially to a peasantry like that of the Lake Country which is in immediate contact with 'the beautiful and permanent forms of nature.' One may make a selection of the real language of men that will be poetical without the addition of any vain ornaments. In other words, the language of verse is not to differ essentially from that of prose.

Wordsworth's views as to the language of poetry varied considerably at different periods of his life and in his actual practice he tended to depart from these views widely at all periods. As an example of a poem that is primitivistic not only in its language, but in its subject one may cite *The Idiot Boy*. This poem is to be read in the light of Wordsworth's letter to John Wilson (Christopher North). The idea of nature, he tells us, had been unduly restricted by a decorum that is not only artificial but heartless. For this exclusiveness based on conventional associations of nobility and lowness we should substitute an all-inclusive sympathy. We shall then be able to develop not only a fellow-feeling for idiots, but even to discover in them an element of sublimity. He is ready to apply to them the phrase of Scripture:

THE PRIMITIVISM OF WORDSWORTH

'Their life is hidden with God.' The idiot in Wordsworth's tale, not being disturbed by his 'meddling intellect,' is able to give himself up to the spontaneous enjoyment of nature. Wordsworth enters sympathetically into this enjoyment; so that Byron is not entirely wrong when he writes

> That all who view the 'idiot in his glory,'
> Conceive the Bard the hero of the story.

By his discarding of conventional decorum in favor of the humble and the lowly the primitivist hopes to achieve not only sympathy and spontaneity but wisdom. Traditionally we have been taught to look up for wisdom to certain great masters of the past, to Christ or Buddha or at the very least to an Aristotle or a Plato. In his poem *Resolution and Independence* Wordsworth tells us that in his moments of spiritual stress he will 'think of the leech-gatherer on the lonely moor.' (It does not appear from Dorothy Wordsworth's *Journal*, by the way, that the leech-gatherer who is the subject of this poem was in real life either 'resolute' or 'independent.')

An even more primitivistic poem than *Resolution and Independence* is *Peter Bell*. The ass in this poem is extolled not only as a suitable object for sympathy, but because he is himself sympathetic and therefore wise. Peter Bell aspires to become wise after the same fashion. He lifts his head — and sees the ass

> Yet standing in the clear moonshine;
> 'When shall I be as good as thou?
> Oh! would, poor beast, that I had now
> A heart but half as good as thine!'

At the end of the poem Peter Bell achieves his wish.

Nature herself is conceived by Wordsworth, not as 'red in tooth and claw,' but as a source of love and pity. In *Hartleap Well* she casts a blight upon the spot that had witnessed the cruelty of the hunters to the hart:

> This Beast not unobserved by Nature fell;
> His death was mourned by sympathy divine.

Even more fundamental in Wordsworth, therefore, than the idea of sympathy is the idea of naturalness and spontaneity. Those who have not yet fallen away from Nature into sophistication possess, one is tempted to say, the artless wisdom of the unconscious. Hence a chief aspect of Wordsworth's primitivism is his cult of childhood:

THE PRIMITIVISM OF WORDSWORTH

Our simple childhood sits upon a throne
That hath more power than all the elements.

According to the associationist philosophy that Wordsworth had adopted, man passes through three periods, each an advance on the last, a progression that Professor Beatty illustrates from the *Ode on Intimations of Immortality*. Unfortunately the poet's heart is not in accord with his head in this matter. One may not, like Señor Madariaga, feel the line 'In years that bring the philosophic mind' as an anti-climax, as 'the most abrupt fall that ever broke the back of an ode,' but it is plain that the poet's heart does not acquiesce in this sober conviction as to the blessings of the philosophic mind. His heart is rather with the vanished spontaneity of the child, 'the hour of splendour in the grass, of glory in the flower.'

One should hasten to add that Wordsworth not only theorizes about spontaneity but often actually achieves it. One cannot read the best of the verse that he wrote during his inspired period without feeling that the contrast between the artificial and the natural that is all-pervasive in the primitivistic movement is something more than a philosophical

[56]

speculation. Matthew Arnold, who has done more than any other one person to mould our conception of Wordsworth, has rightly emphasized this point. His poetry at its best has, he says, the virtue of inevitableness. Arnold has described admirably in his *Memorial Verses* the total effect of Wordsworth's primitivism when it thus receives perfect expression:

> He found us when the age had bound
> Our souls in its benumbing round;
> He spoke, and loosed our heart in tears.
> He laid us as we lay at birth
> On the cool flowery lap of earth,
> Smiles broke from us, and we had ease;
> The hills were round us, and the breeze
> Went o'er the sun-lit fields again;
> Our foreheads felt the wind and rain.
> Our youth returned; for there was shed
> On spirits that had long been dead,
> Spirits dried up and closely furl'd,
> The freshness of the early world.

It is well to remember that in this matter of inevitableness or spontaneity [1] the gap between Wordsworth's best poetry and his worst is abys-

---

[1] Wordsworth himself put great emphasis, not only on spontaneity, but also on conscious art. See his *Letter to a Friend*, Nov. 22, 1831.

mally wide: and even in poems that may seem to some sufficiently inevitable there is room apparently for difference of opinion. Thus Señor Madariaga, whose place among recent Wordsworthian critics is that of devil's advocate, says by way of comment on the ode *To a Skylark* beginning

Up with me! up with me into the clouds! —

'It is the false elation of an elderly clergyman trying to be playful with the schoolboys.' In general, however, Arnold is not only right in praising what is best in Wordsworth's verse for its spontaneity, but he has shown an almost infallible tact in disengaging this truly inspired verse from the mass of uninspired or half-inspired verse in which it is embedded. The weakness of Arnold's essay is its failure to define the quality of Wordsworth's inspiration. Leslie Stephen had praised Wordsworth for his systematic philosophy. Arnold discovers little merit in Wordsworth's systematic philosophy, but at the same time accords him high praise as a critic of life. The systematic and poetically unsound Wordsworth makes a special appeal, he tells us, to the class of persons we should call 'uplifters.'

This whole attempt to distinguish between

THE PRIMITIVISM OF WORDSWORTH

Wordsworth's systematic philosophy, expressed in uninspired verse, and his criticism of life, expressed with poetic inevitableness, will scarcely bear serious scrutiny. On the contrary, Wordsworth is often poetically most admirable in the very passages in which he seems most dubious as a philosopher, or, if one prefers, as a critic of life. At all events, one's views on this subject will be determined by one's attitude towards primitivism. Consider, for example, the two poetically felicitous little poems *The Tables Turned* and *Expostulation and Reply*, perhaps the most extreme expressions of primitivism in English literature, so extreme, indeed, that according to some they are to be interpreted humorously. We are naturally incredulous of any interpretation that involves the ascription to Wordsworth of a sense of humor, especially in view of the fact that the argument of these poems is not so very different from that of other poems that he undoubtedly meant to be taken seriously. Some of the characteristic stanzas of the two poems, it will be recalled, are as follows:

Nor less I deem that there are Powers
Which of themselves our minds impress;

THE PRIMITIVISM OF WORDSWORTH

That we can feed this mind of ours
In a wise passiveness.

.   .   .   .

One impulse from a vernal wood
May teach you more of man,
Of moral evil and of good
Than all the sages can.

Sweet is the lore which Nature brings;
Our meddling intellect
Mis-shapes the beauteous forms of things: —
We murder to dissect.

One may note in passing that the second of these
stanzas, truly Wordsworthian in its inevitableness,
is, considered as a criticism of life, about the most
complete denial of culture in Arnold's sense to be
found in literature. The last stanza brings us back
to the revolt from rationalism in the name of instinct
and feeling of which I have already spoken. Man
should, according to the primitivistic Wordsworth,
unite with Nature, for this union is union with the
Divine. This union is hindered, however, by the
intellect and its importunate analysis, by its tendency to see things, not vitally and synthetically, but
'in disconnection dead and spiritless.' Moreover,
the man who analyzes loses his natural goodness

[60]

and instinctive rightness of feeling. He will presently be ready 'to peep and botanize upon his mother's grave.'

Emotionalism as a substitute for thought is implied, indeed, in Wordsworth's definition of poetry as 'a spontaneous overflow of powerful feelings.' To be sure, Wordsworth adds that the poet should be a man who 'has thought long and deeply,' but read a line or two further and you will find that, following Hartleyan psychology, he looks upon our thoughts themselves as only 'the representatives of all our past feelings.' Coleridge and others who wished to avoid the charge of having substituted emotionalism for thought adopted the nebulous German metaphysical distinction between a higher synthetic reason (*Vernunft*) and the uninspired analytical understanding (*Verstand*). Practically the abdication of the keen discriminations of the understanding, however uninspired, is the abdication of thought. The primitivist has been able to persuade himself of the contrary only by a perversion of the very forms of language, by a twisting of such words as mind and reason from their tried and traditional sense. As an example of this tendency

[61]

one may mention the volume of Mr. F. C. Prescott, *The Poetic Mind.* Mr. Prescott achieves in his view of poetry a sort of blend of Wordsworth and Freud. Mind in its ordinary meaning he turns over to the man of science and the man of business. One becomes creative, on the other hand, and achieves 'poetic mind' only in so far as one surrenders passively to the subconscious stream of imagery.

The kind of revery that results may indeed be poetical; in Wordsworth himself it is often profoundly poetical; but it is precisely in dealing with revery that one needs to display discrimination, true mind, in other words, and not poetic mind in Mr. Prescott's sense. The reputation of Wordsworth either as philosopher or critic of life will finally stand or fall according to the truth or falsehood of a single assumption, namely, that the spiritual life of man has its necessary support in the fresh and vivid perceptions of sense, that each natural object has, in addition to its ordinary meaning, a transcendental significance that makes it relevant to man and his special needs. As a result of this linking of sight with insight the return to Nature of the primitivist takes on the aspect of a

religion. Wordsworth in particular is thus enabled
to declare:

> ... if in this time
> Of dereliction and dismay, I yet
> Despair not of our nature,...
>   ... the gift is yours,
> Ye winds and sounding cataracts! 'tis yours,
> Ye Mountains! thine, O Nature!...

This assertion that the moral ends of man are
forwarded by a union with Nature would seem to
call for the keenest exercise of what Wordsworth
himself terms 'the false secondary power by which
we multiply distinctions.' If we thus discriminate
we may find that the nature cult can assume this
religious aspect only as the result of a confusion
between pantheistic revery and genuine meditation.
Wordsworth himself came to have doubts about
communion with nature as a basis for the moral and
spiritual life of man. At the time of writing the
Ode on Intimations of Immortality, he is already
turning away, though regretfully and with many a
longing, lingering look behind, as I have already
said, from the primitivistic gospel of pure spontaneity. The *Ode* occupies a position in his life somewhat similar to that occupied by the *Ode on*

[63]

THE PRIMITIVISM OF WORDSWORTH

Dejection in the life of Coleridge. The source of Coleridge's melancholy is the discovery that communion with nature is no equivalent for the truths of the inner life:

> It were a vain endeavour
> Though I should gaze forever
> On that green light that lingers in the west;
> I may not hope from outward forms to win
> The passion and the life, whose fountains are within.

The first retreat of Wordsworth on making a similar discovery as to the inadequacy of the gospel of spontaneity is to Stoicism (*Ode to Duty* and *Laodamia*) and then finally to traditional religion (*Ecclesiastical Sonnets*). Our last picture of him is with his white head bowed in the little church at Grasmere. During this last period he not only became the reactionary and 'the lost leader,' but in almost the same measure was forsaken by his muse.[1]

Is it not possible without becoming in any way a reactionary to raise certain doubts about the religious pretentions of the primitivist? Is it not possible, in other words, to discriminate on purely

[1] One should note, however, that Wordsworth wrote four of his best lines — those on Newton in *Prelude* III, 60 ff. — as late as 1839; also that many of the changes in the text of *The Prelude* made late in life are poetically an improvement on the earlier versions.

psychological grounds between pantheistic revery and genuine meditation? In attempting this discrimination we may best fix our attention on Wordsworth's phrase 'a wise passiveness.' We have already seen that the transcendental vision that the primitivist hopes to achieve by communion with nature involves a certain abdication of the intellect. The phrase 'a wise passiveness' raises an even graver problem than that of the intellect, the problem, namely, of the will. It goes without saying that the person who engages in revery is outwardly idle. Is he not also guilty of a far subtler form of idleness? Genuine meditation would seem to differ from revery precisely in the fact that it is a form of effort, a putting forth of a higher will and not merely 'a wise passiveness.'

Why, it may be asked, should we consider matters so curiously? Why not enjoy *Tintern Abbey*, for example, simply as poetry without concerning ourselves about its philosophy? What practical difference does it make after all whether one confuses pantheistic revery with genuine meditation? The answer to this question bears directly on a problem that was Wordsworth's lifelong concern — the problem of happiness. It is all to his credit that in the very age of romantic melancholy, when every poet was trying to outvie his fellow poets in forlornness, in making a 'pageant of his bleeding heart,' he insisted that poets should be the happiest of men. Now it is an impressive fact that the chief religions of the world, notably Christianity and Buddhism, associate happiness not with a wise passiveness but with a wise strenuousness.

Mr. F. C. S. Schiller, of Oxford, recently affirmed that, though we may not have succeeded in adding to the deadly sins, we have at least got rid of some of them — for example, the sin that the mediævals termed *acedia*, which may be defined as the gloom that follows upon spiritual sloth. A sufficiently keen psychological analysis might reveal, quite apart from theological affirmations, that, so far from our having got rid of *acedia*, it is our pet and peculiar failing. Professor Joseph Warren Beach raises a similar issue when he declares that 'Wordsworth on his old gray stone is occupied much like Buddha beneath his sacred Bo-tree,' or like the college professor 'on his summer vacation.' Perhaps the best reply to such an assertion is to quote some characteristic utterance of Buddha — for instance, the following: 'By rousing himself, by strenuousness, by temperance and self-control the wise man may make for himself an island which no flood can overwhelm.'

IV

The problem of happiness is closely related to that of true communion. Arnold cites as an example 'of the noble and profound application of ideas to life' Wordsworth's line:

> Of joy in widest commonalty spread.

There is no doubt that Wordsworth has here formulated felicitously the desirable end. Is it equally certain that he has perceived the means that lead to this end? May one hope to achieve the joy of true communion either through a 'spontaneous overflow' of feeling or through the 'impulse from a vernal wood'? We are all familiar with the admirable lines in which Wordsworth dwells

> On that best portion of a good man's life
> His little, nameless, unremembered acts
> Of kindness and of love.

We do not always recollect that when read in their context these lines contain the suggestion that

[67]

the acts of love may be in no small measure an emanation of the landscape. Similar questions arise regarding the following stanza from the *Song at the Feast of Brougham Castle:*

> Love had he found in huts where poor men lie;
> His daily teachers had been woods and rills,
> The silence that is in the starry sky,
> The sleep that is among the lonely hills.

This is one of the most perfect expressions of primitivism to be found in any language. Here if anywhere 'Nature herself seems (in Arnold's phrase) to take the pen out of Wordsworth's hand and to write for him with her own bare, sheer, penetrating power.'

But, it may be objected, can one dismiss the first line of the stanza as merely primitivistic? Is it not in accord with the side of the Gospel that looks forward to Saint Francis and his praise of poverty? That wealth and high station are beset with spiritual perils is beyond question. One may also grant that Lord Clifford was fortified against these perils by much that he had learned during the years he had spent as a shepherd. The suggestion of the line that is Rousseauistic rather than religious is that the poor abound in love simply because they are poor. Religion does not estimate the presence or absence of love or of any other virtue on a collective basis but solely in terms of the individual. Rousseau, on the contrary, so builds up the contrast between the hard-heartedness of the rich and great and the innate goodness of the poor as to encourage the class war; and the class war is not Christian. Furthermore, if we are to judge by the remaining lines of the stanza supported by other passages that I have quoted or might quote, Wordsworth's 'love' derives, like Rousseau's 'pity,' not from some higher source but from 'nature.' The ideas of sleep and silence and loneliness are all primitivistic rather than religious. Religion does not take refuge in sleep (or the unconscious) but holds out to man the hope of a true awakening. It opposes to loneliness a communion based on a wisdom transcending all that one may learn from 'woods and rills.' The Christian in particular associates his wisdom not with silence but with the divine Word. The cult of silence, to be sure, is not always primitivistic but calls in any case for close scrutiny. Does Carlyle, for example, speak as a primitivist or as a

wise man in his voluble celebration of silence?
There is no room for doubt when Alfred de Vigny
proclaims that 'silence alone is great — all the rest
is weakness'; for the line is part of a passage in
which he avers that man should, in his mode of
dying, emulate the wolf.

Wordsworth affirms paradoxically that grace, by
which alone man can, according to the Christian,
become capable of rising above Nature, is on the
contrary the only means by which he may unite
with Nature:

> ... By grace divine,
> Not otherwise, O Nature! we are thine.

The danger of this scheme of salvation is that it
may lead to the setting up of a subrational parody
of the charity that is at the heart of genuine Christianity and which traditionally has been inseparable from grace.

An interesting comparison may be made at this
point between Milton and Wordsworth. Both men
had solemnly dedicated themselves to poetry, but
with a difference. The poetic excellence at which
Milton aimed was to be achieved, he tells us, only
'by devout prayer to that eternal Spirit, who can

enrich with all utterance and knowledge, and sends out his seraphim with the hallowed fire of his altar to touch and purify the lips of whom he pleases.' The dedication of which Wordsworth was conscious was inspired in him by the contrast between a country dance he had been attending and its incidents, on the one hand, and, on the other, 'all the sweetness of a common dawn.'[1] This consecration to a Spirit that is in nature is surely not the same as Milton's to a Spirit that transcends it.

A main divergence between the two consecrations would seem to be as to the source of love. The 'Nature' of Wordsworth and other primitivists which both feels and inspires love, which offers in short the equivalent of the 'order of charity,' is evidently not nature as known to the realistic observer, but an idyllic dream. Practically this means that, if one is to arrive at a sound estimate of Wordsworth, one must deal not only with his attitude towards the intellect and the will, but must also define the quality of his imagination. The word imagination may be applied first of all, as it has been ever since the Greeks, to the various impressions of sense

[1] *Prelude*, IV, 309–38.

which are in Wordsworth's case often admirably vivid (especially the visual impressions). It does not follow that the wonder of natural appearances which he has rendered with such success can take the place of the homage of awe and reverence and humility that we owe to that within us which transcends natural appearances. The union with nature as something essentially religious which both Wordsworth and Coleridge made the basis of their distinction between fancy and imagination must therefore be itself dismissed as fanciful. Wordsworth himself contrasts two types of imagination — on the one hand, the 'enthusiastic and meditative,' and on the other 'the human and dramatic'; and he evidently includes himself among the poets who are enthusiastic and meditative in the quality of their imagination. The epithets enthusiastic and meditative would seem to apply especially to a poet like Dante, but his enthusiasm and meditation are surely not on the whole of the same type as Wordsworth's. Unlike him Dante is primarily not an idyllic but a religious poet; as a Christian he is preoccupied above all with the problem of man's will both in itself and in its relation to God's will. Nothing could be more foreign to the true spirit of the *Divine Comedy* than the doctrine of a wise passiveness.[1] Dante is not merely a greater poet than Wordsworth — so much I think we should all grant — but if the distinctions I have been attempting are just, it would follow that his superiority is not merely one of degree but of kind.

It is plain that if Wordsworth's imagination is not, on the whole, of the religious type, it is even less of the type that he himself terms human and dramatic. Perhaps no great poet ever saw life less dramatically than Wordsworth. The sonnet on London seen from Westminster Bridge is not only successful, it is splendidly successful. At the same time there is a certain element of paradox in treating a great city as a study in still life. To take another instance, the subject of *The White Doe of Rylstone* would seem to call for a direct portrayal of the clash of human wills and the violent deeds that

[1] According to certain extreme Christians, man should be passive to God's will — something very different from being passive to an 'impulse from a vernal wood.' According to moderate Christians, there should be coöperation between the divine will and man's.

[73]

result; on the contrary Wordsworth is not content until he has converted the whole situation into 'emotion recollected in tranquillity.' *The Excursion* has claims to be regarded as the least dramatic long poem in literature. Its crowning incident, as has been remarked, is 'tea at the vicarage.' [1] Just as I have expressed the opinion that Wordsworth differs by the quality of his vision or imagination from a religious poet like Dante, so I venture to affirm that he differs from poets like Shakespeare and Sophocles, who are imaginative in the human and dramatic way, not merely in degree but in kind. Other things being equal, a poet who dwells imaginatively on the humanistic or the religious level seems to deserve a higher rating than the poet who is engaged imaginatively in a return to nature.

---

[1] There is no doubt again that *Michael* is a perfect poem of its kind. The question as to what this kind is has been answered by Wordsworth himself in his sub-title: *A Pastoral Poem*. Michael is not guilty of any fault or error of will such as has been associated traditionally with genuine tragedy. Here as in the almost equally admirable *Margaret* episode in the first book of *The Excursion*, Wordsworth is aiming at a sort of *katharsis* of tears for *undeserved* affliction — a notion of *katharsis* that he seems to have derived from certain sentimentalists of the eighteenth century. See *Sentimental Morality in Wordsworth's Narrative Poetry* by Oscar J. Campbell (*University of Wisconsin Studies in Language and Literature*, No. II).

THE PRIMITIVISM OF WORDSWORTH

'Last and pre-eminently,' says Coleridge, 'I challenge for this poet (i.e. Wordsworth) the gift of IMAGINATION in the highest and strictest sense of the word.' Coleridge has been followed in this view by so many and such weighty authorities that, in suggesting that Wordsworth's imagination is not after all of the highest type, I am, like Dr. Johnson in his attack on the three unities, appalled by my own temerity.

The critic, it is true, cannot afford to be exclusive. According to Anatole France, pantheism is the most poetic of all ways of viewing life. One may at least admit that Wordsworth and other primitivists have shown that it may be abundantly poetical. Moreover Wordsworth cannot be dismissed as a merely pantheistic poet. He is guilty at times of the 'egotistical sublime' of which Keats accused him, but at other times he achieves the elevation that is the mark of a truly religious spirit — an elevation that he often proceeds to associate more or less arbitrarily with 'the light of setting suns,' or the equivalent. In general it is not unusual for the great romantics to combine flashes of genuine insight with pantheistic revery. There is an especially baffling mixture of this kind in a writer who was influenced in a notable degree by Wordsworth — our own Emerson. In one poem he declares that there are 'two laws discrete not reconciled — law for man and law for thing.' In another poem he assures us that the humble bee is 'wiser far than human seer,' an example of 'immortal leisure.' As we approach the present the insight diminishes and the pantheistic confusion grows. I choose a few illustrations almost at random. Not long ago one of the leading Protestant pastors of Boston expressed his sense of religion by having placarded in front of his church the following lines by W. H Carruth:

> A haze on the far horizon,
>   The infinite, tender sky,
> The ripe, rich tint of the cornfields,
>   And the wild geese sailing high —
> And all over upland and lowland
>   The charm of the golden rod —
> *Some of us call it Autumn,*
>   *And others call it God* [my italics].

In his volume, *The Modern Dilemma*, Mr. Hugh I'Anson Fausset makes a plea 'for a true reconciliation of heart and head in imaginative under-

standing, a true at-one-ment with the spiritual
source and reality of all being, by virtue of which
nature is perceived as supernatural and the *life of
a flower is in its degree as beautiful and inevitable a
mystery as the life of Jesus'* [my italics]. The
primitivist seeks at times to dissimulate his spiritual
idling under grandiose imagery:

> Oh, subtle is the sap athrill,
>   Athletic is the glad uplift,
> *A portion of the cosmic will,*
>   *I pierce the planet drift* [my italics].

Primitivism of this kind may do very well as a
week-end and holiday attitude. It can be received
as serious philosophy only at the expense of a certain quality of will and imagination. In his *A Cycle
of Modern Poetry* Professor G. R. Elliott has
pointed out with admirable perspicacity how this
quality of will and imagination is compromised
by Wordsworth's virtual denial of the mysterious
duality of human experience in favor of a single
life that 'rolls through all things.' If the poet, he
says, is to learn once more to see life either religiously or dramatically, he needs to turn from
Wordsworth to Milton and the Elizabethans at

their best — for example, to the Shakespeare of
Macbeth. Without denying the validity of the
avenue of escape that Professor Elliott offers the
poet from what he terms 'the dying orbit of the
nineteenth-century mind and art,' it is well to
remember that the problem we are here concerned
with is, before being a poetical, a human one,
and that it is possible to deal with this problem
not merely traditionally, but critically, or, what
amounts to the same thing, to affirm the higher will
for which the primitivist offers a subrational substitute, as a living and present perception.

Wordsworth is 'well pleased to recognize in
nature and the language of the sense' the 'guide'
and 'guardian' of all his 'moral being.' Saint
Bonaventura, though very ready on occasion to
interpret religiously natural appearances, yet affirms finally that 'the soul knows God without the
support of the outer senses.' Here, if anywhere, is a
clash of first principles. If there is to be any recovery of the truths of the inner life it may be
necessary to work out some positive psychological
equivalent of the form of immediacy implied in the
utterance of Saint Bonaventura, and then oppose it

THE PRIMITIVISM OF WORDSWORTH

to the Wordsworthian immediacy. I have in mind of course the needs of those persons who are unable simply to acquiesce in traditional authority and who yet see the peril of naturalistic confusion. The first and most urgent task of those who wish to escape from this confusion in truly modern fashion would seem to be to rehabilitate the 'secondary power' of discrimination that Wordsworth so disparaged, in other words, to develop a more trenchant type of criticism.

III

THE PROBLEM OF THE IMAGINATION: DR. JOHNSON

As is well known, the imagination was under suspicion during the neo-classical period. This suspicion extended far beyond the bounds of literature in the narrower sense and was variously grounded. Philosophers like Descartes and Spinoza objected to the imagination because it was an obstacle to truth, a truth which, as they conceived it, was to be achieved by abstract reasoning. The imagination was also attacked, especially by Pascal, in the name of religion. According to Pascal, the imagination is a 'proud power,' a 'mistress of error,' which overwhelms the reason in which the philosophers put their trust. Man can hope to escape from the deceits of imagination only by a divine succor, the illumination of grace. The imagination is at times attacked on both rationalistic and religious grounds as, for example, by Malebranche in his *Recherche de la Vérité*.

The hostility of the literary critics of the period to

DR. JOHNSON AND IMAGINATION

the imagination has somewhat different grounds. Though, like the philosophers, they oppose 'reason' to imagination, by reason they mean not so much abstract reasoning as intuitive good sense. By intuitive good sense one may determine what is normal or 'probable' and so achieve centrality in one's point of view. Imagination, on the other hand, tends to pull one off center. For example, false wit is, according to La Bruyère, eccentric wit; and it is eccentric, because 'it has too much imagination in it.' Dr. Johnson echoes many predecessors when he declares the imagination 'a licentious and vagrant faculty, unsusceptible of limitations, and impatient of restraint.' This distrust of the imagination can be explained historically as a recoil not only from the school of conceits but also from the extravagance of the mediæval type of fiction, as it appears in the romances of chivalry. The neo-classicist was at times all the more hostile to this type of fiction in that he had personally experienced its perils. According to Bishop Percy, Johnson 'when a boy was immoderately fond of reading romances of chivalry and he retained his fondness for them through life... Yet I have heard him attribute to these extravagant fictions that unsettled turn of mind which prevented his ever fixing in any profession.'

A movement looking to the rehabilitation of the imagination got under way in the eighteenth century and gained ground with surprising rapidity in view of the extent of the previous distrust. The important period in this movement is that which extends from the publication of Addison's papers on the imagination in *The Spectator* (1712) to Young's *Conjectures on Original Composition* (1759). It was at this time that the phrase 'creative imagination' or 'creative fancy' began to gain currency. If it could be shown that Dr. Johnson shared this new attitude towards the imagination there might be some justification for affirming with a recent writer that 'he was an important motive force behind that tidal wave of revolt which eventually was to engulf the outworn creed (of neo-classicism).' On the contrary, Johnson displays the full neo-classic suspicion of the imagination, combined at times with a type of suspicion that reminds one of Pascal. On the other hand, he has little or nothing of the distrust of the imagination, based on an overweening faith in abstract reason, that one finds in a Descartes or a

DR. JOHNSON AND IMAGINATION

Spinoza. As a preliminary to understanding his attitude, one needs to distinguish between two main meanings of the word 'imagination' in the period that preceded him. As used by the philosophers, the word refers to the various impressions of sense or else to a faculty that stores up these impressions. When Hobbes, for example, defines imagination as 'decaying sense,' he is still very close to the conception of fancy (*phantasia*) set forth by Aristotle in his *Psychology*. The literary critics, on the other hand, often use the word imagination in a sense that derives, not from Aristotle's *Psychology*, but from his *Poetics*. Aristotle, it will be remembered, does not employ the word 'fancy' or 'imagination' at all in the *Poetics*. What the neo-classic critic was later to call imagination he there describes as 'fable' or 'myth' or 'fiction.' The right relationship, according to Aristotle, between the truth that the poet can give us and fiction is of crucial importance for our whole subject. The poet, he tells us in a familiar passage of the *Poetics* (Chapter IX), is superior to the historian because the truth that he gives us is less implicated than that of the historian in the particular. Homer is the greatest of poets, he adds in Chapter XXIV, because he has the most of this general truth and his success in achieving it is due to the fact that he is the most accomplished of liars.

Critics during the neo-classic period, as well as more recently, seem to have found it singularly difficult to grasp this Aristotelian conception of representative fiction, of truth through illusion. From Robortelli, who published his commentary on the *Poetics* in 1548, to the present day, they have tended on various grounds to put their truth or reality in one compartment and their fiction or illusion in another. One may illustrate the neo-classic form of this tendency from Dr. Johnson. He never tires of telling us that poetry should aim not at the particular but at the general. He does not as a rule, however, associate his general truth with a right use of fiction or, if one prefers, with a certain quality of imagination. On the contrary, instead of dwelling on a possible coöperation between truth and fiction, he inclines to set the two in sharp opposition to one another. According to Hawkins, 'he could at any time be talked into a disapprobation of all fictitious relations, of which he would frequently say they took no hold of the mind.'

He was especially unwilling to admit any relation between fiction and religious truth. Like Boileau he therefore rejects the Christian epic because it introduces fiction into a domain where truth alone is appropriate. 'The good and evil of Eternity,' he says, 'are too ponderous for the wings of wit.'

Though Boileau would have religious truth and fiction sharply segregated, he encouraged fiction in one of the main senses that the word had come to have in the neo-classic period — the use, namely, of the pagan myths. Johnson, though in general sympathy with Boileau, breaks with him sharply at this point. 'The rejection and contempt of fiction (i.e., fiction in the sense of the classical myths) is,' he says, 'rational and manly.' Granted that classical fiction had become intolerably trite in the hands of minor poets, one is inclined to ask whether Johnson felt sufficiently how profoundly poetical this fiction had once been, nay, how poetical it may still be, if employed imaginatively. We do not think of him as striving that he might

> Have sight of Proteus rising from the sea;
> Or hear old Triton blow his wreathéd horn.

Towards another main type of fiction Johnson

was implacable — namely, the type that appears in the pastoral. He would have none of it even in a Milton. He sickened at the mere mention of lambs and shepherds' crooks and was especially angered, we are told, by any praise of the Golden Age. Here again one may grant all that Johnson says about the more factitious forms that the pastoral theme had assumed and at the same time ask whether he does justice to the poetry of which the pastoral is capable. No classicist can afford to follow Schiller in his *Essay on Simple and Sentimental Poetry*, and grant the first place to the idyllic imagination; at the same time he must recognize that man is never perhaps more spontaneously imaginative than when he yields to his Arcadian longings. 'Turn where you will in mythology and literature,' says Mr. P. E. More, 'and you will find this pastoral ideal haunting the imagination of men.... Were one to attempt to display its universality by illustration, one would need to abridge the libraries of the world into a few pages.'

The idyllic imagination was assuming a new importance in the time of Johnson as a result of its association by Rousseau and other primitivists with a state of nature to which men were actually invited to return. More or less innocent illusion was thus being converted into dangerous delusion. Dr. Johnson not only failed, as it seems to me, to do justice to the poetry of pastoral fiction; he also failed — though, in view of his condemnation of Rousseau, it is not possible to speak so confidently on this point — to perceive its full peril. The pastoral dream to which the princess succumbs in *Rasselas* is of the conventional rather than of the new primitivistic type.

Of the peril of fiction in general, of the ease with which illusion passes over into delusion, Johnson was only too acutely conscious. Chapter 43 of *Rasselas* on 'The Dangerous Prevalence of Imagination' not only gives the key to this work, but, taken in connection with *Rambler 89* on 'The Luxury of Vain Imagination,' points to one of Johnson's constant preoccupations. The neo-classic distrust of the imagination is, as I have already said, reinforced in him by that of the Christian. Traditionally, however, the Christian has been more inclined than was Johnson to invite a man to enter into himself. The man who enters into himself may achieve true meditation instead of becoming the puppet and plaything of vain conceits. It is this latter possibility that

Johnson seems to take too exclusively into account. He himself rather dreaded being alone. He appears to have been happier when drinking tea with Mrs. Thrale. He associated with his solitary moments the fits of 'hypochondriac obnubilation' to which, as he tells us, he was subject. There is no evidence that he cultivated in a notable degree 'that inward eye which is the bliss of solitude' in the sense that a Christian saint would have given to the phrase 'inward eye.' In the sense that Wordsworth gave to the phrase Johnson did not of course cultivate the inward eye at all. 'Solitude,' he says, 'is a state dangerous to those who are too much accustomed to sink into themselves.' In his account of the 'recluse' who regales himself with 'airy gratifications,' who yields to 'an invisible riot of mind,' who is unable to distinguish between the 'labor of thought' and 'the sport of musing,' Johnson anticipates admirably much of our modern psychology. 'The dreamer,' he says, 'retires to his apartments, shuts out the cares and interruptions of mankind, and abandons himself to his own fancy; new worlds rise up before him, one image is followed by another, and a long succession of delights dances round him. He is at last called back to life by nature, or by custom, and enters peevish into society, because he cannot model it to his own will.'

This passage, written in 1751, runs curiously parallel to the passage in the *Confessions* in which Rousseau narrates how in 1756 at the Hermitage he made of his 'creative imagination' a means of escape into a 'land of chimeras' and how rudely he rebuffed visitors who interrupted him at the moment when he was on the point of setting out for '*le monde enchanté.*' In this particular use of the creative imagination Rousseau has had innumerable followers. The person who indulges in this quality of fiction is termed by the psycho-analyst in his own special jargon, the 'introvert' or victim of 'autistic' thinking. Johnson does not fall into the pseudo-scientific fallacies of psycho-analysis, especially in his dealing with the problem of the will. He does, however, remind one at least remotely of the psycho-analyst by the remedy he proposes for the maladjustment that grows out of the flight from the real into some world of fiction. He puts his emphasis on outer activity rather than on the inner activity by which Christian and Aristotelian alike would adjust themselves to a higher reality, an adjustment that Aristotle relates specifically in the *Poetics* to a right use of fiction or illusion.

One should add that though Johnson was in general very prone to see illusion passing over into delusion, he refused to admit any such passage precisely at the point where most neo-classic critics discovered it — namely, in the type of drama that conformed to the three unities. It is well known that the doctrine of the three unities arose in Italy during the sixteenth century and was imposed on the European drama in connection with the Quarrel of the Cid. In the name of pseudo-probability, the illusion of a higher reality that true tragedy requires is converted by this doctrine into literal deception. Various attacks on the unities had been made in the eighteenth century before Johnson, one of the earliest being by a French writer, La Motte-Houdard, who is in his total tendency pseudo-classical. To those familiar with these previous attacks on the unities the attack in the *Preface to Shakespeare* (1765) will not seem especially original. There is no doubt, however, that Johnson's refutation of the idea of literal deception is masterly and

definitive. Towards the end of this refutation he
suggests that there may be other and better reasons
for observing the unities than those based on a false
verisimilitude. As a matter of fact, the unities have
been revived in our own day, largely through the
influence of Ibsen, because they have been found
to make for concentration, a prime requirement of
good dramatic technique. The larger question of
verisimilitude in the Aristotelian sense still remains
unsolved. A melodrama may observe the unities or
approximate them and in other respects display excellent dramatic technique, and yet remain wildly
improbable, because its action is not motivated
with reference to normal human experience. It is
not enough to make a plea as Farquhar already does
in his attack on the unities in his *Discourse upon
Comedy* (1702) for 'a free and unlimited flight of
imagination.' The value of the imagination that is
thus free to 'wander wild,' that is not in other words
disciplined to any norm, is precisely the problem
raised by the whole modern movement. Critics contemporary of Dr. Johnson complained that, though
he had shown that we are not actually deluded at a
play by the observance of the unities or by any

other device, he did not do justice to the degree of illusion that a play may actually produce — for example, when he says that a 'play read affects the mind like a play acted.' What is certain is that he did not bring together adequately the idea of fiction or illusion and the idea of verisimilitude. As I have been pointing out, he tends, like most neo-classic critics, to set imagination and reason (or judgment), illusion and verisimilitude, in sharp opposition to one another. The contrast that he establishes in *Rasselas* is between a merely deceitful fancy and 'sober probability.' Unfortunately, there is truth in the assertion of observers so different as Pascal and Napoleon that imagination governs mankind. Anyone who wishes, therefore, to make a right appeal to men will not be satisfied with opposing cool reason or judgment to imagination but rather one quality of imagination to another. Johnson indeed has an occasional remark of admirable perspicacity regarding the mechanical opposition between judgment and imagination that runs through the neo-classic movement. 'It is ridiculous,' he says, 'to oppose judgment to imagination; for it does not appear that men have necessarily less of one as they have more of the other.'¹ If he had developed adequately the hint he has thus thrown out, if he had done justice to the rôle of fiction or illusion in both life and art, if he had linked with a right use of the imagination, the 'grandeur of generality' that he is always opposing to what seems to him every deviation from normal human experience, the romantic rebels would have been left without any legitimate grievance. As it was, these rebels simply took over the neo-classic opposition between reason and imagination and turned it upside down. Instead of sacrificing imagination to reason, they were ready to sacrifice reason to what A. W. Schlegel calls the magic of genuine illusion.

If there is to be any important advance in criticism at the present time a first step would seem to be to overcome the neo-classic and romantic opposition between reason and imagination and seek to recover the Aristotelian idea of a coöperation between the two. A preliminary investigation should be made of the different meanings that have been given the word 'imagination,' not merely by the literary critics

¹ Under the date Sept. 18, 1760, Johnson enters in his Journal the somewhat enigmatical resolve, 'To reclaim imagination.' See *Johnsonian Miscellanies*, edited by G. B. Hill, vol. I, p. 25.

but by the philosophers and psychologists from the Greeks down. Since the time of Johnson, one may note in passing, the task of defining imagination has been complicated by the transformation of the word attempted by Wordsworth and others at the beginning of the nineteenth century. As M. Legouis remarks acutely, 'Wordsworth claimed imagination as his supreme gift, but at the same time he bestowed on the word "imagination" a new meaning, almost entirely opposed to the ordinary one. He gave the name to his accurate, faithful, and loving observation of nature. In his loftier moods, he used "imagination" as a synonym for "intuition," of seeing into, and even through, reality, but he never admitted a divorce between it and reality. The gift of feigning, or arbitrarily combining the features of a legend or story, which had long been held to be the first poetical prerogative, was almost entirely denied him, and he thanked God for its absence.'

I have already suggested that the 'nature' of Wordsworth and other primitivists is in no small measure a projection of the idyllic imagination and in so far is not 'real' in any sense of that much-abused word. At all events, it is not yet clear that the type of imagination by which one is enabled, according to Wordsworth, to enter into communion with 'nature' is more important than the type that he dismisses so disdainfully, the type that M. Legouis describes as 'the gift of feigning, of arbitrarily combining the features of a legend or story.' One should add that this type of imagination cannot afford to be entirely arbitrary, if it is to meet the Aristotelian requirement of probability; it must in short be disciplined to normal human experience. In proportion as it is thus disciplined it gains in reality in the humanistic and not in the current naturalistic sense. Persons are still found sufficiently naïve to suppose that the word 'romantic' is specially hard to define as compared with other general terms like 'real,' 'ideal,' 'nature,' 'imagination.' As a matter of fact, a certain integrity has been maintained in the use of the word 'romantic' in spite of a bewildering multiplicity of specific applications. What was called romantic in the Middle Ages is still romantic, whereas, in the case of the word 'real'[1] in particular, there have been

[1] God was for the mediæval schoolman *ens realissimum*. It is hardly necessary to comment on the contrast between this use of the word and the present one.

since the mediæval period radical changes of meaning. An urgent task, if we wish to escape from our present confusion, is therefore to define above all the words real (or realism) and imagination, not only separately but in their relation to one another. If definition of the kind I have in mind is carried out with sufficient thoroughness, the way may be opened for the theory and possibly the practice of that art of representative fiction to which Johnson, in spite of his genuine humanistic wisdom, does not seem to me to have done entire justice, and to which even less justice has been done in the movements that have succeeded one another since his day.

IV

THE PROBLEM OF THE IMAGINATION: COLERIDGE

A STRIKING feature of the whole modern movement has been its passion for origins. Tendencies that in other respects diverge widely agree in the assumption that, not the end as Aristotle asserts, but the beginning is 'the chief thing of all.' One may detect at least this likeness between the man of science who scoffs at the very idea of final causes and seeks to get back to electrons or chromosomes, and the primitivist who has a predilection for 'art's spring-birth so dim and dewy' and sets 'the budding rose above the rose full blown.' We no longer believe in the nobility of the savage, but still hope, under the obsession of evolutionary theory, to derive our chief enlightenment regarding the human race itself from an endless prying into pre-history. Similarly, in dealing with the individual, we delve in the depths of the subliminal self and incline to interpret maturity in terms of childhood. Here again the backward glance is a bond between points of view that, at first sight, seem utterly dissimilar. At the very age, for example, when the child is hailed by Wordsworth as 'mighty prophet, seer blest,' he is most likely, according to Freud, developing an 'Œdipus complex.'

This passion for origins has been especially conspicuous for several generations past in both the creation and the critical study of art and literature. It has at last made possible a work like the recent important volume on Coleridge by Professor John Livingston Lowes.[1] The search for sources — in this case the sources of *The Ancient Mariner* and *Kubla Khan* — has perhaps never been carried on more competently. In tracking Coleridge's immense and recondite reading Professor Lowes has displayed an industry little short of prodigious. He has claims to be regarded as the most accomplished of literary sleuths. He has devoted well over four hundred pages of his book to building up the background of two short poems, not to speak of a hundred and fifty pages of notes which are, in his own phrase, 'securely kenneled in the rear.' Moreover,

[1] *The Road to Xanadu, A Study in the Ways of the Imagination* (Houghton Mifflin Company, 1927).

he does not mean that his investigation should cater merely to learned curiosity. He has related it to another main preoccupation of our time — that with subliminal psychology — in the hope of thus throwing light on the mystery of the creative imagination itself.

Professor Lowes distinguishes three stages in the creative process. The first stage is conscious: the fixing of the attention on some particular field and the accumulation of material that bears upon it. In the second and, it would seem, essential stage the material thus accumulated sinks into the region of the subliminal self and there enters into new and unexpected associations. Professor Lowes seeks to show how in *The Ancient Mariner* and *Kubla Khan* the images that Coleridge had derived from his multifarious reading, especially of books of travel, were thus magically modified in the 'deep well of unconscious cerebration.' The view of creative genius that has been popular ever since the eighteenth century has encouraged emphasis on the unconscious and the spontaneous, more or less at the expense of the purposeful. Thus Ruskin writes of Turner: 'He only did right when he ceased to reflect; was powerful only when he made no effort, and successful only when he had taken no aim.' In much the same vein Emerson declares of the Parthenon and the Gothic cathedrals: 'These temples grew as grows the grass'(!). Even the partisan of a pure spontaneity cannot, however, if one is to believe Professor Lowes, afford to be ignorant. An ample preliminary enrichment of the mind is desirable, if only that the unconscious may have something to work upon.

The third stage of the creative process recognized by Professor Lowes is, like the first, conscious. However magically the material supplied by the unconscious may have been modified, it is still more or less inchoate. It is only by an effort, deliberate though still imaginative, that it can be fashioned into a harmonious whole. The 'shaping spirit of imagination' has thus presided over *The Ancient Mariner*, whereas it is absent from *Kubla Khan*. This latter poem may indeed be regarded as the most notable example in literature of creation that has not got beyond the second stage; at least if one accept the usual belief, based on Coleridge's own statements, that it came to him precisely in its present form as a fragment of an opium-dream.

One may grant that Professor Lowes's account of the 'ways of the imagination' is relevant to the two poems he has studied and yet ask if he has not exaggerated its general relevancy. He says in his preface that he does not propose to consider whether *The Ancient Mariner* is classic or romantic or whether it meets the Aristotelian test of high seriousness. Actually, he has answered these very questions by implication in the body of the book when he mentions the poetical Coleridge in the same breath with Homer, Dante and Milton and uses the phrase 'supreme imaginative vision' in connection with *The Ancient Mariner*. My own endeavor will be to show that the imagination displayed in *The Ancient Mariner* is qualitatively different from that displayed in poetry that may rightly be regarded as highly serious. The whole problem has an importance transcending Coleridge and his influence, far-reaching though that influence has been. The imagination, as Pascal puts it, disposes of everything — even of religion, to an extent that Pascal himself would probably have been loath to admit. The importance of the subject is, however, equaled only by its difficulty. The chief difficulty is that 'imagination' belongs to a class of words, unhappily tending to increase, that have been used in so many meanings that they have almost ceased to have any meaning. One's first temptation is simply to banish words of this type from one's vocabulary. A saner precedure is to strive for more accurate definition, definition which, if it is to be valid, should be based first of all on a broad historical survey of what the general term under consideration actually has meant.[1]

What one discovers in dealing in this fashion with the word imagination is that it has in the past been used primarily to describe the various impressions of sense or else a faculty that was supposed to store up these impressions. It therefore gives only appearances and not reality. Here is a main source of the persistent suspicion of the imagination that can be traced from early Greek times to the eighteenth century. When Saint Bonaventura, for example, says that the 'soul knows God without the support of the outer senses' he merely means to affirm that

[1] Useful material will be found in *The Theory of Imagination in Classical and Mediæval Thought* (1928) by M. W. Bundy. A second volume is promised that will cover the modern period.

man is not dependent for his perception of religious truth on the imagination.

The association of imagination or phantasy with mere appearance no doubt explains why Aristotle does not employ the word at all in his *Poetics*. For poetry, he tells us, that is to be accounted highly serious, must penetrate beyond the impressions of sense to the universal. To be sure, this universal is not achieved directly, but only with the aid of 'myth' or fiction. Moreover, the art of representative fiction, as Aristotle conceives it, is intensely dramatic. To imitate the universal means practically to depict human actions not at random but with reference to some sound scale of ethical values. Centrality of vision is necessary if poetry is to have 'probability,' if, in other words, it is to disengage true unity and purpose from the welter of the actual. But though Aristotle's prime emphasis is in poetry and elsewhere on purpose, he recognizes man's almost insatiable craving for the marvelous. The more wonder the better, he seems to say, provided it does not involve an undue sacrifice of truth to the universal. Tragedy that has with the aid of representative fiction or significant illusion suc-

ceeded in portraying the universal through the particular, tends to raise the spectator to its own level
and, as a result of this enlargement of spirit, to re-
lieve him of what is merely petty and personal in his
own emotions. This is the true *katharsis* that Milton has, with the intuition of a great poet, rendered
so admirably at the end of *Samson Agonistes*.

I have been pointing out in my essay on Johnson
that the neo-classic theorist made much of imitation and probability, but tended to divorce them
from fiction in the sense of illusion; that fiction in
this sense had come to be associated with certain
forms of romantic extravagance; and that one of
the reasons for the distrust of the imagination was
its identification with a one-sided quest of wonder.
Yet Voltaire himself had declared that 'illusion is
the queen of the human heart.' The neo-classic
inadequacy at this point was a chief factor in the
rise of the romantic movement, a movement
marked at its inception, as I have said, by the
appearance of a new phrase, the 'creative imagination.' This creativeness was associated not with
imitation but with spontaneity, which came to
mean practically emotional spontaneity. Further-

more the movement speedily took on a primitivistic coloring.

The eighteenth-century theorists of originality and genius thus prepared the way for Wordsworth's definition of poetry as 'the spontaneous overflow of powerful feelings,' and for the closely related idea that this overflow is most likely to be found in peasants and other simple folk who are still close to 'nature.' Wordsworth, however, goes beyond the earlier primitivists by reinterpreting, largely it would seem under the influence of Coleridge, the word imagination. Imagination in the older sense of fiction, whether probable or improbable, he disparages. He himself lacked what he terms the 'human and dramatic imagination,' but felt he had something better in the 'enthusiastic and meditative imagination.' The imagination to which he accords his homage is not only 'Reason in her most exalted mood,' but the faculty that enables one, in contradistinction to the more or less arbitrary associations of mere 'fancy,' to achieve a true spiritual unity, not to be sure immediately but mediately through the objects of sense. For the Wordsworth of *Tintern Abbey*, God is, in M. Legouis's phrase, a

'gift of the senses,' a position radically opposed to
that which appears in the sentence of Saint Bonaventura I have just quoted. Wordsworth has coined
for his imaginative blending of himself with the
landscape the phrase 'a wise passiveness.' But can
one regard this imaginative blending as meditative?
Genuine meditation requires effort. One may speak
properly of the *act* of recollection but not of the act
of revery; and it is pantheistic revery that *Tintern
Abbey* plainly encourages. At all events, a striking
feature of Wordsworth's poetical theory and, to no
small degree, of his practice, is his dissociation of the
imagination from effort or action in either the ordinary dramatic or the religious sense.

For the relationship he establishes between sight
and insight and the resulting facility with which he
reads a transcendental significance into the 'mean-
est flower that blows,' Wordsworth was, as I have
said, indebted to Coleridge, who was in turn indebted to the Germans; though as to the exact
extent of the indebtedness in either case it is well
not to be too dogmatic. One would therefore have
anticipated that Coleridge in his treatment of imagination and kindred topics in the *Biographia Lit-*

eraria would be in accord with Wordsworth. Coleridge would not, however, be the baffling figure he is if such were entirely the case. In the earlier chapters of this work he does indeed set out to define imagination in a way that would apparently have confirmed Wordsworth at essential points, but tends to get lost in what he himself terms 'the holy jungle of transcendental metaphysics.' One is reminded by all this portion of the *Literary Life* of Carlyle's inimitable account of Coleridge's conversation at Highgate: if anyone asked him a question, Carlyle reports, instead of answering it, or decidedly setting out towards an answer of it, he would 'accumulate formidable apparatus, logical swim-bladders, transcendental life-preservers and other precautionary and vehiculatory gear for setting out.' After much preparation of this kind in the *Literary Life*, he seems in chapter thirteen to be getting under way at last; but just at this point someone writes him a letter (the someone as we know now was Coleridge himself) warning him that he is getting beyond the depth of his public and advising him to reserve his more recondite considerations for his work on the Logos (which was of course never written). Whereupon Coleridge turns from Schelling and the Germans to Aristotle.

The result of this escape from the 'jungle' is a sudden increase in clarity. There arises out of the transcendental haze one of 'the balmy sunny islets of the blest and the intelligible' that, according to Carlyle, also emerged at times in Coleridge's conversation. Indeed the chapters in which Coleridge deals on Aristotelian grounds with the paradoxes into which Wordsworth had been betrayed by his primitivism constitute the chief islet of this kind to be found in his prose writings. Thus (if I may be pardoned for summarizing material so familiar) Coleridge, having laid down the principle that poetry requires an 'involution of the universal in the individual' proceeds to apply this principle to *The Excursion*. Wordsworth has in this poem put sublime philosophic discourse in the mouth of a peddler. Some particular peddler may be sublime, Coleridge retorts, but peddlers as a class are not sublime. The peddler of *The Excursion* is a possible but not a probable peddler. Again, a child of six who is a 'mighty prophet' can scarcely be regarded as a representative child. Coleridge objects

in like Aristotelian fashion to Wordsworth's assertion that the true language of poetry is to be found
on the lips of dalesmen who enjoy the advantage of
contact with the 'beautiful and permanent forms of
nature.' Excellence of speech, Coleridge replies in
substance, is a product of conscious culture. So far
as the dalesmen possess it, it has come to them, not
as an emanation of the landscape, but as a result
above all of their reading of the Bible. Wordsworth
was right in rejecting the 'gaudiness and inane
phraseology' that had arisen from the imposition on
poetry of the artificial decorum of a social class.
But there is a true as well as an artificial decorum.
Though the poet should eschew mere polite preju-
dice, he cannot afford to neglect in his choice of
words their conventional associations, as Wordsworth, a recluse with a defective sense of humor,
was at times too prone to do. The intrusion of
words with trivial associations into serious verse
will produce on readers the effect of 'sudden and un-
pleasant sinkings from the height to which the poet
had previously lifted them.' Wordsworth is also
guilty at times of a somewhat different type of in-
decorum — namely of using 'thoughts and images

too great for the subject.' This latter type of disproportion Coleridge terms 'mental bombast.'

Though Coleridge's critique of Wordsworth is thus Aristotelian in its details, transcendentalism would seem to reappear in its conclusion; and transcendentalism is a doctrine that mixes about as well with that of Aristotle as oil with water. 'Last and preëminently,' he says, 'I challenge for this poet [i.e., Wordsworth] the gift of IMAGINATION in the highest and strictest sense of the word.' If Coleridge had been a more thorough-going Aristotelian, he might have found that the chief source of 'mental bombast' in Wordsworth arises from the disproportionate significance that he had been led by his transcendental philosophy to attach to natural appearances; when, for example, he exclaims, on his discovery of the small celandine, that he will 'make a stir, like a sage astronomer.' The stir would seem justified only in case it could be shown that, through imaginative communion with the small celandine, he attained a real spiritual unity. But what proof is there of the reality of a communion achieved in that way? One may perhaps best reply in the words of Coleridge:

COLERIDGE AND IMAGINATION

> Oh, William, we receive but what we give
> And in our life alone does nature live.

In that case the nature with which one communes is not nature as known to the impartial observer but merely a projection of one's own mood on outer objects — in other words, a form of the pathetic fallacy. It follows, as I have remarked in a previous essay, that the unity thus achieved is not real but fanciful, so that the distinction between imagination and fancy that both Wordsworth and Coleridge strove to establish breaks down at the center.

Compared with the poetry that portrays action through the medium of fiction with reference to normal experience, communion with nature of the transcendental sort would appear to be only a new and fascinating mode of escape. The need of escape is deep-seated and universal and has been satisfied in manners manifold in the literature of the past. One would not, indeed, err greatly in choosing as epigraph for about nine tenths of this literature these lines of Emily Dickinson:

> I never hear the word 'escape'
> Without a quicker blood,
> A sudden expectation,
> A flying attitude.

COLERIDGE AND IMAGINATION

The chief instrument of escape is the imagination — a certain quality of imagination. One need not quarrel with imagination of this quality when it shows itself frankly for what it is. It becomes dubious only when put at the basis of what purports to be idealism or even religion. This form of self-deception has flourished especially in connection with our modern return to nature. Thus Rousseau writes: 'My soul wanders and soars in the universe on the wings of imagination in ecstasies that surpass every other enjoyment.' The results that follow from indulging this type of imagination are scarcely of a kind to satisfy either the humanist or the man of science. The wandering and soaring, they would agree, are for the most part, not in the universe, but in the tower of ivory. Similarly the 'liberty' and 'intensest love' to which Coleridge lays claim as a result of 'shooting his being through earth, sea and air' are accomplished only in dreamland. Like the Wordsworth of *Tintern Abbey*, Coleridge is setting up in this passage of *France: An Ode*, pantheistic revery as a substitute for true meditation.

This is not of course the whole truth about either

COLERIDGE AND IMAGINATION

Wordsworth or Coleridge. Wordsworth attains at times to a truly religious elevation. In associating this elevation, however, with the 'light of setting suns' or some other aspect of outer nature, he is encouraging a confusion between spiritual and æsthetic perception. As a matter of fact, the first person who seems to have done justice æsthetically to the light of setting suns is 'the notorious ribald of Arezzo,' Aretino (letter to Titian, May, 1544).

There is, again, in Coleridge an element of genuine religious vision. He seems singularly different, however, in the total impression he produces, from the religious teachers of the past. These teachers, whether a Saint Bernard or a Buddha, are as energetic and purposeful as the head of some great industrial enterprise in our own time, though, one scarcely need add, in an entirely different way; whereas one can scarcely find in the whole annals of literature another personality so richly endowed as Coleridge and at the same time so rudderless. According to the familiar anecdote, he could not even determine which side of the garden walk would suit him best, but corkscrewed back and forth from one side to the other. There is more here than the ordinary contrast between the willingness of the spirit and the weakness of the flesh. His irresoluteness is related in at least some measure to his primitivism — above all to his notion that genius is shown primarily in a capacity for sinking 'back again into the childlike feeling of devout wonder.' It is no doubt true, as Mencius remarked long ago, that the great man is he who has not lost his child's heart; but it is also true that greatness appears in the power to impose on life a masculine purpose. It is not easy to estimate the precise proportion of primitivistic to genuinely religious elements in Coleridge himself. Regarding his major influence, it is possible to speak more confidently. This influence has, in Walter Pater's phrase, been a 'part of the long pleading of German culture for the things behind the veil.' Practically this has meant an interest in the elusive phenomena that are off the center of normal consciousness; the very phenomena, in short, to which Professor Lowes had devoted so much attention. As a result of his preoccupation with these crepuscular regions Coleridge impressed at times those who approached him as almost somnambulistic.[1] The picture Peacock has drawn of him in *Nightmare Abbey* with his curtains drawn at midday and sprinkling salt on the candle to make the light burn blue has at least the truth of caricature.

This interest in the abnormal was by no means confined to Coleridge. It has been said of his age in general that it 'grovelled in the ghastly and wallowed in the weird.' Such an age had in *The Ancient Mariner* its appropriate masterpiece. In its psychology and incidents and scenic setting it marks the extreme sacrifice of the verisimilar to the marvelous. It is at a far remove from the Aristotelian high seriousness, which not only requires relevancy to normal experience but a relevancy tested in terms of action. Apart from the initial shooting of an albatross the Mariner does not do anything. In the literal sense of the words he is not an agent, but a patient. The true protagonists of *The Rime of the Ancient Mariner*, Professor Lowes remarks rightly, are the elements — 'Earth, Air, Fire and Water in their multiform balefulness and beauty.' As Charles

[1] Cf. the title of the recent volume by J. Charpentier: *Coleridge, The Sublime Somnambulist.*

COLERIDGE AND IMAGINATION

Lamb puts it: 'I dislike all the miraculous part of the poem, but the feelings of the man under the operation of such scenery dragged me along like Tom Piper's magic whistle.' Between a poem like *The Ancient Mariner* in which the unifying element is feeling and a poem which has a true unity of action the difference is one of kind; between it and let us say *The Fall of the House of Usher* the difference is at most one of degree. In this and other tales Poe has, like Coleridge and indeed partly under his influence, achieved a unity of tone or impression, a technique in short, perfectly suited to the shift of the center of interest from action to emotion.

Intense emotion, especially under the stress of a unique experience, is isolating. Perhaps no work embodies more successfully than *The Ancient Mariner* the main romantic motif of solitude. ('Alone, alone, all, all alone!') Here if anywhere the soul is a state of the landscape and the landscape a state of the soul — the outer symbol of a ghastly isolation. The mood of solitude based on the sense of one's emotional uniqueness is closely interwoven, again, as every student of the modern movement knows, with the instinct of confession. Rousseau himself says of certain childhood experiences: 'I am aware that the reader does not need to know these details but I need to tell them to him.' In much the same fashion the Wedding Guest does not need to hear the Mariner's tale, but the Mariner needs to relate it to him. The psycho-analysts have, with rare effrontery, applied to the relief that results from a yielding to the confessional urge the noble term *katharsis*. It should be apparent that the term cannot be applied in its correct meaning to mere emotional overflow nor again to fiction in which wonder and strangeness prevail so completely, as in the present case, over imaginative imitation of the universal.[1]

It follows from all that has been said that *The*

---

[1] Professor Lowes says that '*The Rime of the Ancient Mariner* is as normal as the *Odyssey*' in virtue of 'the ways of the imagination that underlie them both.' (*Road to Xanadu*, pp. 425, 426.) One may reply that, though there is no lack of the marvelous in the *Odyssey*, its excellence as a poem is due primarily to its centrality of vision, to the success with which it portrays imaginatively normal human nature *in action*. The Ancient Mariner, on the contrary, has been described as only an embodied memory. What he remembers is so abnormal that the Wedding Guest doubts with some reason whether he is a human being at all. The pilot's boy goes 'crazy' merely from having witnessed the closing incident of the Mariner's voyage.

COLERIDGE AND IMAGINATION

Ancient Mariner, judged by the quality of the imagination that informs it, is not only romantic but ultra-romantic. One should not therefore disparage it, or in general regard as the only test of poetry its degree of conformity with the model set up by Aristotle in his *Poetics*. One must insist that in the house of art are many mansions. It does not follow that the mansions are all on the same level or of equal architectural dignity. That *The Ancient Mariner* is good in its own way — almost miraculously good — goes without saying. The reason for thinking that this way is inferior to the way envisaged by Aristotle is that it is less concerned with moral choices in their bearing on the only problem that finally matters — that of man's happiness or misery. Professor Lowes's praise will seem pitched in too high a key to anyone who accepts this or some similar scale of poetical values. He himself is not quite consistent at this point. At one moment he agrees with Coleridge that the fiction of the poem should have been openly irresponsible like that 'of the Arabian Nights' tale of the merchant's sitting down to eat dates by the side of a well, and throwing the shells aside, and lo! a genie starts up, and says he *must* kill the aforesaid merchant, *because* one of the date shells had, it seems, put out the eye of the genie's son.' In general Professor Lowes seems to dismiss the whole demand for probability as worthy only of literary philistines like Mrs. Barbauld, who complained, it will be remembered, of *The Ancient Mariner* that it was 'improbable and had no moral.'

At other moments, though recognizing the grotesque disproportion between the Mariner's initial act and its consequences, Professor Lowes seems to take the tale seriously as a treatment of the great drama of guilt and expiation.[1] The fact is that it is impossible to extract any serious ethical purport from *The Ancient Mariner* — except perhaps a warning as to the fate of the innocent bystander; unless indeed one hold that it is fitting that, for having sympathized with the man who shot an albatross, 'four times fifty living men' should perish in torments unspeakable.

In the meanwhile, contrary to Mrs. Barbauld's assertion, *The Ancient Mariner* actually has a moral ('He prayeth best, who loveth best,' etc.). Moreover, this moral, unexceptionable in itself, turns out,

[1] *The Road to Xanadu*, p. 298.

when taken in its context, to be a sham moral. The mode in which the Mariner is relieved of the burden of his transgression, symbolized by the albatross hung about his neck — namely, by admiring the color of water-snakes — is an extreme example of a confusion to which I have already alluded: he obtains subrationally and unconsciously ('I blessed them *unaware*') the equivalent of Christian charity. Like many other works in the modern movement, the poem thus lays claim to a religious seriousness that at bottom it does not possess. To this extent at least it is an example of a hybrid and ambiguous art.

By turning their attention to the wonder and magic of natural appearances Wordsworth and Coleridge and other romantics opened up an almost inexhaustible source of genuine poetry. Wonder cannot, however, in this or in any other form serve as a substitute for the virtues that imply a something in man that is set above the phenomenal order. If we are to believe the great teachers of the past, the pathway to religious wisdom does not lie through the flower in the crannied wall or the equivalent. The attempt to base religion on won-

der becomes positively grotesque when Walt Whitman declares that 'a mouse is miracle enough
to stagger sextillions of infidels.' The underlying
confusion of values has, however, persisted in less
obvious forms and is indeed the most dubious legacy
to our own time from the romantic age. Thus Mrs.
O. W. Campbell asserts that 'Christ was the first
romantic and the greatest.'[1] According to Mr.
Middleton Murry, again, when a person does not
dare to come out and attack Christ openly he vents
his spleen on Rousseau.[2]

The distinction between two entirely different
orders of intuition that is being blurred or obliter-
ated by the writers I have just been citing is closely
related to the problem of the imagination. Perhaps
no recent critic has spoken more wisely on the
nature of this relationship than a French contemporary of Coleridge — Joubert; and that at the
very time when Coleridge was insinuating that 'a
Frenchman is the only animal in the human shape
that by no possibility can lift itself up to religion or
poetry.' Joubert not only displays the same high

[1] *Shelley and the Unromantics*, p. 252.
[2] See *Criterion*, vol. VII, p. 78.

type of vision that appears at times in Coleridge but he has the advantage over Coleridge of not being addicted either to opium or German metaphysics. The most important distinction made by Joubert is that between an imagination that does not rise above the impressions of sense and an imagination that gives access to the supersensuous, that is, in short, an organ of insight. It is only with the aid of this latter type of imagination that one achieves the 'illusion of a higher reality'; the illusion is indeed, according to Joubert, 'an integral part of the reality.'

One cannot afford to disdain in the creative process what may be termed the spontaneities, all that seems to come as a free gift, for example, the magical combinations and permutations of images in the 'deep well.' Coleridge, however, falls into a dangerous primitivistic exaggeration when he says that 'there is in genius itself an unconscious activity; nay, that is the genius in the man of genius.' The imagination that Joubert calls the 'eye of the soul' is fully conscious and also creative, though in a different sense: it creates values. It does so by coöperating with reason in the service of a higher will. The unconscious activities must be controlled with reference to the values thus created with the help of the ethical imagination, as one may term it, if they are to have direction and purpose, in other words human significance. Technique is admittedly something that must be consciously acquired. The question of the ethical imagination is, however, plainly one that concerns not merely the technique or outer form of creative work, but its inmost essence.

Failure to make some such distinction as that I have been attempting, exposes one to the risk of confounding work that has abundant human substance with work that has little or none. Serious confusions of this kind are rife at the present time — more serious indeed than any with which Professor Lowes may be properly charged. For example, Mr. E. E. Kellett writes in his recent volume *Reconsiderations*: 'There is something in the very choice of subject which marks out the *supreme* poet from his fellows. It is not an accident that Coleridge chose to write of *diablerie* and witchcraft.... The fact that Chaucer's subjects are in the main of the earth, earthy, is significant of the limits of his poetic genius.'

COLERIDGE AND IMAGINATION

It may be maintained that Dante has a depth of religious insight that puts him definitely above Chaucer. But to accord to romantic *diablerie* the same rating as to religious insight and to dismiss Chaucer, one of the most human of poets, as 'of the earth, earthy' in comparison with the Coleridge of *The Ancient Mariner*, is surely inadmissible. Here and elsewhere in his volume, Mr. Kellett reminds one of the French partisans of 'pure poetry.' So much is eliminated by the Abbé Bremond,[1] the chief spokesman for this group, as not being of the essence of poetry, that it is, like Jowett's idea of God, in danger of being defecated to a pure transparency. Poetry becomes a *je ne sais quoi*, an 'electricity,' an indefinable magic that is similar, the Abbé Bremond would have us believe, to the mysterious and impalpable something that is present in the attitude of prayer. The truth is that the Abbé is ready to make an abject surrender of conscious discrimination and control in favor of a pure spontaneity, with a resulting confusion of the subrational with the superrational and finally of romanticism with religion

[1] See his volumes *La Poésie pure* and *Prière et poésie* (1927).

[124]

that, in so prominent a churchman, is positively disconcerting.

The sacrifice of human substance to the Moloch of spontaneity is even more manifest in the contemporary French group known as the 'super-realists' (*surréalistes*), affiliated in their point of view with the English and American writers who abandon themselves to the 'stream of consciousness.' The very name that the members of this group have assumed would indicate that they are in error as to the direction in which they are moving. What they term 'reality' is plainly not above but below the human and rational level. The upshot of the quest of creative renewal in this region would appear to be, if one may judge from some of the contributions to *transition*,[1] the organ of the group, a sort of psychic automatism.

I am not going too far afield in speaking of the *surréalistes* apropos of Coleridge. If a poem like *The Pains of Sleep* anticipates Baudelaire, *Kubla Khan*, as I have already remarked, probably remains the best example of a spontaneity that, so far from having been disciplined to either humanistic

[1] Now defunct.

or religious purpose, has not even undergone any technical shaping of the kind one finds in *The Ancient Mariner*. It illustrates what Coleridge himself calls the 'streamy nature of association' in revery at least as well, and far more agreeably, than, let us say, the closing pages of Joyce's *Ulysses*.

The notion that one becomes creative only by being spontaneous is closely related to the notion that one becomes original only by being unique. If we are to judge by *surréalisme* and other recent literary cults the time is approaching when each writer will, in the name of his genius conceived as self-expression, retire so completely into his own private dream that communication will become impossible. To be sure the drift of these recent cults towards sheer unintelligibility marks a violent extreme of the kind that usually comes towards the end of a movement. It is an extreme, however, that points to a one-sidedness in the movement from the start — the tendency, namely, to exalt the differences between man and man and to disparage or deny the identities. The result has been a fatal confusion between individuality and personality. True personality is not something that, like individuality, is bestowed upon a man simply because he has taken the trouble to be born. It is something that he must consciously win with reference to a standard set above his merely temperamental self; whereas there has probably never been a blade of grass, which, if it become vocal, might not say truthfully, in the language of Rousseau, that, if not better than other blades of grass, at least it was different. The notion that one may become creative simply by combining temperamental overflow with a greater or lesser degree of technical skill has resulted in work that often displays genius indeed but suffers at the same time from a taint of eccentricity; work in which, in Aristotelian parlance, the wonderful quite overtops the probable. Anatole France writes of Victor Hugo, perhaps the extreme example of genius of the eccentric type: 'One is saddened and at the same time frightened not to encounter in his enormous work, in the midst of so many monsters, a single human figure.... He wished to inspire wonder and long had the power to do so, but is it possible always to inspire wonder?'

The doctrine of imitation, setting up as it does some standard with reference to which a man must humanize his gift, whatever that gift may chance to be, is, in all its forms, chastening; perhaps, in some of its forms, too chastening. One remembers the prostration of the literary aspirant before the models during the neo-classic period. On the other hand, the doctrine that discredits imitation in favor of spontaneity does not put a man sufficiently on his guard against what Buddha and other sages have declared to be the two root diseases of human nature — conceit and laziness. It would not be difficult to find modern applications of a sentence that was written by Robert Wolseley as long ago as 1685: 'Every ass that's romantic believes he's inspired.'

But to return to Coleridge: at his best, especially when he insists that great poetry must be representative, he can scarcely be charged with having encouraged the over-facile type of inspiration. One may ask however whether he has brought the doctrine of representativeness, with its inevitable corollaries of imitation and probability, into sufficiently close relation with his actual defining of the imagination and its rôle. The most famous of his critical phrases, 'that willing suspension of disbelief for the moment, which constitutes poetic faith,' does not

[128]

appear to afford any adequate basis for discriminating between poetic faith and poetic credulity. The fact that a fiction of any kind is enthralling is no sure proof that it has human substance. Otherwise certain detective stories would merit a high literary rating. The phrase was actually framed with a view to justifying *The Ancient Mariner*, a tale that lacks probability, not only in Mrs. Barbauld's sense, but, as I have been trying to show, in Aristotle's as well. Nor is it enough to speak of 'the shaping spirit of imagination,' for the imagination may shape chimeras. One cannot again be wholly satisfied with the definition of 'the primary imagination' as 'a repetition in the finite mind of the eternal act of creation in the infinite I AM.' This would seem to be an invitation to the romantic to exalt himself to the level of deity before making sure of the validity of his imaginings apart from his own emotions.

We must conclude therefore that, in spite of many admirable remarks by the way, Coleridge does not succeed in disengaging his theory of the imagination sufficiently from the transcendental mist. It is to be regretted above all that he did not affirm clearly the rôle of the imagination in giving access to a supersensuous reality; an affirmation that is necessary if the doctrine of imitation and probability is to be relieved of every suspicion of formalism. Instead, he inclined to see the highest use of the imagination in Wordsworth's communing with natural appearances, and so became one of the promoters of the great pathetic fallacy that has been bewildering the human spirit ever since.

Wordsworth, who tended to read into the landscape what is not there (for example, 'unutterable love'), at the same time that he rendered, often fortunately, the wonder that is there, disparaged science. Yet probably the chief reason for the comparative eclipse of the imagination that seizes what is normal and central in human experience in favor of the imagination that yields to the lure of wonder has been the discoveries of science. These discoveries have engendered an intoxication with novelty for which the past offers no parallel. The modern man has been kept on the tiptoe of expectation by one marvel after another. For the moment he is thus imaginatively enthralled by the conquest of the air. He is infinitely removed from the Horatian *nil admirari*, even though he does not set out deliberately, like a certain French minor poet, to 'live in a state of bedazzlement.' As a result of the interplay and coöperation of the various forms of naturalism, the attitude of the modern man towards life has become purely exploratory — a sheer expansion of wonder and curiosity. He cannot even conceive another attitude. Yet a situation is gradually growing up that may force him to conceive it. Wonder has a large place in the scheme of things, but is after all only a sorry substitute for the law of measure of the humanist or for the religious virtues — awe, reverence and humility.

If one wishes to understand how humanism and religion have been more or less compromised by the modern movement with its 'Renascence of Wonder,' it is still helpful to go back to its earlier stages. Matthew Arnold expressed the opinion that the burst of creative activity in English literature through the first quarter of the nineteenth century had about it something premature. Whatever justification there may be for this opinion is found in the failure of the romantic leaders to deal critically enough with the idea of creation itself. The doctrine of creative spontaneity towards which they inclined, though in the case of Coleridge with reservations, suffered, as I have been trying to show, from a one-sidedness that has persisted to the present day. Unless this one-sidedness is corrected, it is to be feared that art and literature will be menaced with a more than Alexandrian decline. As a matter of fact, Joyce's *Ulysses*, which has been saluted by Miss Rebecca West, speaking for no inconsiderable portion of the younger literary set, as a work of 'majestic genius,' marks a more advanced stage of psychic disintegration than anything that has come down to us from classical antiquity. If there is to be any recovery of humanistic or religious truth, at least along critical lines, it would appear desirable to associate the creative process once more, not with spontaneity, but with imitation, imitation of the type that implies a supersensuous model imaginatively apprehended. According to the late Stuart Sherman, 'the great revolutionary task of nineteenth-century thinkers was to put man into nature. The great task of twentieth-century thinkers is to get him out again.' Superficially, the most serious danger of the primitivistic immersion of man in nature to which Sherman refers is that it leads to a denial of reason; a still graver danger, one finds on closer scrutiny, is that it leads to an obscuring of the true dualism — that between man's natural self and a higher will — or more frequently to the setting up of some subrational parody of this will such as one finds in *The Ancient Mariner*. The obscuring of the higher will has coincided practically with the decline of the doctrine of divine grace with which it has in the Christian Occident been traditionally associated. The issues involved evidently extend far beyond the boundaries of literature. But, to consider literature alone, it would seem necessary to recover in some form, perhaps in a purely psychological form, the true dualism, if creation is once more to be achieved that deserves to be accounted highly serious — creation, in other words, that is informed by the human and dramatic quality of imagination.

V

SCHILLER AS ÆSTHETIC THEORIST[1]

It is no light task to trace the total influence of Schiller on the romantic movement. A French scholar, M. Eggli, has recently managed to write two octavo volumes — over thirteen hundred closely printed pages! — simply on the French phases of this influence.[2] He is especially copious on Schiller's influence upon the French drama, both romantic and pre-romantic. Many of the romantic plays that borrowed motifs from Schiller may be defined as parvenu melodramas. But through *The Robbers* — and Schiller was long known not merely

[1] In May, 1920, Professor Arthur O. Lovejoy published in *Modern Language Notes* a review of my volume *Rousseau and Romanticism* in which he accused me of misrepresenting Schiller's æsthetic ideas. I replied to this review in an article in the same publication (May, 1922) entitled *Schiller and Romanticism* to which Professor Lovejoy appended a rejoinder: a few passages from my article in *Modern Language Notes* appear in the present essay. My references are to the tenth volume of the Goedeke edition of Schiller.

A translation of Schiller's æsthetic treatises will be found in the Bohn Library. I have in a few cases used the Bohn rendering in my citations.

[2] *Schiller et le Romantisme français* par Edmond Eggli (1927).

to France but to the rest of Europe almost entirely as the author of *The Robbers* — he promoted, as M. Eggli has shown, the rise of the actual melodrama. *Robert Chef de Brigands*, loosely adapted from *The Robbers* by La Martelière, with the help, it would seem, of Beaumarchais, had an instantaneous success (March 10, 1792). The thrills it provided were, even more obviously than in Schiller's play, in the service of revolutionary passions. After *Robert Chef de Brigands* had been running six months the Legislative Assembly bestowed upon Schiller the title of French citizen. A copy of the printed decree signed by Danton and Clavière, and accompanied by a letter from the minister Roland was dispatched to Germany in October, 1792, addressed to 'M. Gille, German publicist.' These documents, now in the library at Weimar, did not reach Schiller until 1798. All the men who had signed them had perished victims of the Revolution long before, so that his diploma of French citizenship, as Schiller said, seemed to come to him from the empire of the dead.

According to Goethe, the dominant idea in Schiller's writing is that of liberty — only this idea underwent a progressive purification. At the outset indeed Schiller embodies in an extreme form the two main aspects of the revolutionary spirit, an expansive, not to say an explosive liberty, as in *The Robbers*, and an equally expansive sympathy — a sympathy so inclusive that Schiller is ready to 'embrace the millions' and 'bestow a kiss upon the whole world.'

Schiller was not, however, permanently satisfied with the more naïve forms of the revolutionary dualism. Largely under the influence of Kant, he came to be concerned with the conflict between good and evil not merely in society but also in the individual. His attitude towards this conflict, as it appears in his philosophical treatises, can scarcely be said to mark a return to either the Christian or the classical point of view. He is almost as ready as Rousseau himself to see in decorum not a vital principle but the mere 'proprieties' of a degenerate neo-classicism. Nor is there again any necessary connection between Christian humility and Kant's conception of the practical reason that Schiller adopted. The freedom that one may achieve by obeying the categorical imperative is scarcely to be identified with 'the glorious liberty of the children of God.' At the same time the way by which Schiller would have man escape from his inner disharmony is not entirely Kantian. Kant seemed to him too harsh and uncompromising. He was, he said, the Draco of his age, because it had shown itself unworthy of having a Solon. On strictly Kantian lines indeed Schiller seemed to himself to be caught between two necessities — on the one hand, the necessity of the moral law; on the other, the necessity of nature. This is the dilemma with which he has dealt especially in his *Æsthetic Letters* and his essay on *Grace and Dignity*. He seeks for immediacy not in the supersensuous to which Kant denies him direct access, but in emotion. He chooses appropriately as epigraph for his *Æsthetic Letters* a sentence of Rousseau: 'Si c'est la raison qui fait l'homme, c'est le sentiment qui le conduit.' He sets out to solve æsthetically and emotionally the problem of dualism — the strife of which man is conscious between his higher and his lower nature. There can be no doubt as to the importance of this problem. If we were to agree with M. Eggli that Schiller's solution of it is satisfactory, we should have to conclude that he is one of the greatest sages of all time. There has been, however, from the start a singular diversity of judgment regarding the value of Schiller as an æsthetic theorist. In his Conversations with Eckermann (14 November, 1823), Goethe speaks of Schiller's 'unblest days of speculation.' 'It was sad to see how so highly gifted a man tormented himself with philosophical disquisitions which could in no way profit him.' [1] In our own day M. Victor Basch sums up an elaborate study of Schiller's æsthetic theories as follows: 'We do not believe that either the method or the premises or the conclusions of Schiller's poetics are truly valid.' My own estimate of the value of Schiller's æsthetic theories is very similar to that of M. Basch, only I would base it on very different reasons. The whole subject, it must be confessed, is one of extreme difficulty. The full elucidation of it would require a volume. I can hope here to touch on only a few of the main issues.

It is hardly possible to make clear what these issues are without passing rapidly in review the background of Schiller's philosophical treatises. I

[1] Goethe does not seem always to have thought so unfavorably of Schiller's Kantian speculations. See *Kant, Schiller, Goethe,* von Karl Vorländer. (Zweite Auflage, 1923.)

have pointed out elsewhere in this volume that there was during the neo-classic period a failure to do justice to the imagination and its rôle in art and literature. This neo-classic tendency was reënforced by the rationalistic dryness of the Enlightenment (*Aufklärung*). As the German romantics later complained, the *Aufklärer* were for building bake-shops on the slopes of Parnassus. They wished, to change the metaphor, to put Pegasus in harness.[1] In order that Pegasus might once more soar into the empyrean two forms of emancipation seemed necessary, one of the imagination, the other of the emotions. The first form of emancipation, as I have remarked in another essay, can perhaps best be traced in connection with the rise of the phrase 'creative imagination.' Regarding the second form of emancipation it is well to remember that epithets like sentimental and æsthetic not only have etymologically an identical meaning but that Shaftesbury, though he does not use either epithet, actually merges the æsthetic and the sentimental. He can scarcely be said to discriminate between the moral sense and the sense of beauty. The conduct of the

[1] See Schiller's poem *Pegasus in der Dienstbarkeit.*

man who indulges his instinctive affection for his fellows will be at once beautiful and ethical. Shaftesbury may be regarded as a precursor not only of all the benevolists but of all the æsthetes of the last two centuries. Shaftesbury's disciple Hutcheson, however, while continuing to affirm the close connection between the moral sense and the sense of beauty, sought to justify the latter independently. At the same time English empiricists were seeking to eliminate from the idea of beauty the abstract and intellectual element that Leibniz and others had discovered in it, and to base it entirely on sensation. This empirical element is very visible, for example, in Burke's *Inquiry into the Sublime and Beautiful.* In France the Abbé Dubos especially was insisting on the rôle of sensibility in one's notion of the beautiful. The way was being prepared, in short, for the setting up of æsthetics as a separate subject. The work that is supposed to mark the definite emergence of this new subject, the *Æsthetica* of Baumgarten (1750), grants however less to the purely sensuous element in beauty than one might infer from the title.

The work that sums up and presupposes the æsthetic theorists I have been mentioning — on the one hand, intellectualists like Leibniz, and, on the other, sensationalists like Burke—and at the same time looks forward to most subsequent speculations in this field is Kant's *Critique of Æsthetic Judgment.*[1] Kant also reveals the influence of theorists like Gerard, Duff, Young, Home, etc., who, though they often do lip service to good taste and judgment, are in the main on the side of the autonomous or 'creative' imagination and the emancipated sensibility; who are, in short, preparing the age of genius. This influence is apparent when Kant says, for example, that all are agreed that genius is incompatible with imitation or when he denies genius to the man of science on the ground that he does not enjoy sufficient freedom of imagination. At the same time Kant is repelled by the type of imaginative and emotional freedom that was beginning to appear in the Storm and Stress.

Kant remains indeed in the final analysis a rationalist, and, one may add, an extraordinarily difficult one. Anyone who has struggled through the metaphysical maze of the *Critique of Æsthetic Judg-*

[1] First part of *The Critique of Judgment.* English translation with useful references to Kant's English predecessors by J. C. Meredith (1911).

ment is likely to agree with Joubert that it is possible to sprain one's mind as well as one's body. The complications of Kant's argument are due largely to his assertion that æsthetic judgments have universal validity, and at the same time to his effort to put this universality, as he was forced to do by his general philosophy, on an apriorist and intellectualistic basis. We may at least sympathize with M. Victor Basch in his somewhat diffuse volume on the æsthetics of Kant,[1] that there is nothing abstract in our estimates of beauty: they are invariably based on something immediate. M. Basch is on more doubtful ground when he goes on to affirm that because beauty is necessarily a 'sentiment,' it therefore excludes the idea of the universal. If one is to avoid the reduction of beauty to the purely relative, one needs to oppose to M. Basch's 'sentiment' another form of immediacy — the perception namely of something that abides in the midst of the phenomenal and the transitory, and is indissolubly bound up with it. This abiding oneness is of many orders. The constant factors in human nature itself,

[1] *Essai Critique sur l'Esthétique de Kant.* (Deuxième édition augmentée, 1927.)

as something distinct from physical nature, ought, one might suppose, to be of special interest. I have sought to describe elsewhere in this volume the coöperation of imagination and analytical reason by which one may hope to grasp these constant factors and in that sense attain to reality, even though this reality fall far short of being absolute. By this coöperation it is possible to build up a pattern of normal experience that one may imitate. Imagination and reason thus coöperate, according to Matthew Arnold, in the great Greek poets: the effect produced by the poetry of Sophocles, for example, is that of 'imaginative reason.'

One may ask, however, whether imagination and reason are likely to work together perfectly save in subordination to a higher power. Some such question is forced upon one by Kant's æsthetic theory both in itself and in its influence upon Schiller. Kant assumes this higher power — a quality of will peculiar to man that is, he declares, grounded in the supersensible. At the same time he denies that man has direct access to this supersensible or noumenal realm. The sharp divorce that Kant establishes between the noumenal and the phenomenal involves

him in extraordinary difficulties, especially in dealing with the idea of freedom. As a phenomenon
among other phenomena man may, Kant admits, be
strictly determined and at the same time in the
noumenal realm be perfectly free! Kant evidently
raises in an acute form in all three of his Critiques
the question of intuition. In *The Critique of Æsthetic
Judgment* one is led to inquire whether one may not
have a direct perception of the universal; in *The
Critique of Practical Reason*, whether one must base
one's conduct on a categorical imperative that remains a mere abstraction; in *The Critique of Pure
Reason*, whether, craving as one does immediacy,
one must be put off with the 'unearthly ballet of
bloodless categories.' One may, to be sure, go to the
opposite extreme. 'Would to heaven,' says Pascal,
'that we never had need of reason, and that we
might know all things by instinct and sentiment.'
Even the pure traditionalist can scarcely afford to
speak so disparagingly of reason; still less the person
who sets out to be critical. Even though one reduce
reason to a secondary and instrumental rôle, one
still needs to retain it, as I am fond of repeating, if
only to discriminate between different orders of in-

tuition. One should beware, as I point out in my Introduction, of confounding Pascal's use of the word sentiment to designate a higher will, with Rousseau's use of the same word to designate expansive emotion. One may insist, I have said, on the element of psychological truth in Pascal's 'sentiment' quite apart from the theology with which Pascal and other Christian supernaturalists have been wont to associate it.

Granted that a man may have the direct intuition that Kant denies him of a higher or ethical will, the question recurs whether his imagination and reason are likely to coöperate in the way I have described, without some degree of subordination to this will. A closely related question is whether great art and literature are possible apart from supernatural religion. It has been maintained that the supernatural has always been present in some form, at least in the background, of great art.[1] It is well not to be too affirmative on this point. In much art and literature of the past of a high, though not perhaps of the highest type, the religious element is not conspicu-

[1] See article by P. E. More: 'A Revival of Humanism' in *The Bookman* (New York), April, 1930.

ous. It is not easy, for example, to discover in Molière's plays what Mr. More terms 'the glamour of the supernatural.' Moreover there is evidence that Molière was positively unfriendly, not only to the Christianity in his own background, but to supernaturalism in general.

Our present topic, however, does not call for a full discussion of this difficult question as to the relationship between religion and great art. It is enough to note, as I have already done, that the harshness of a categorical imperative or ethical will that does not rest on anything immediate led Schiller to take refuge in a merely emotional immediacy. On his own showing, as we shall see more fully in a moment, imagination and reason do not coöperate under this new hegemony of feeling.

The neo-classicist, to be sure, had also failed on the whole to achieve a coöperation between imagination and reason. There is an historical explanation, as I have sought to show in my essay on Johnson, for the neo-classical tendency to disparage unduly the imagination in favor of 'reason,' 'judgment' or the like. The dryly analytical type of 'Enlightenment' that still had many representatives in

Schiller's day, also failed to do justice to the rôle of the imagination. The problem would seem to have been to give the imagination greater scope without emancipating it from direction and purpose, or, what will be found to amount to the same thing, without loss of the idea of the universal. It is difficult to see how one can retain this idea and at the same time proclaim like Kant that genius and imitation are incompatible. It appears to follow that a man has genius only in so far as his imagination is not subordinated to any end, only in so far as it is allowed to play freely. In effect Kant is one of the chief sponsors for the so-called play theory of art. At the same time, though he conceives of the freedom of the imagination in terms of play, he is unwilling to admit that it is *irresponsible* play. He therefore seeks to show by dint of metaphysical subtleties that art may have a purpose which is at the same time not a purpose (*Zweckmässigkeit ohne Zweck*). In much the same fashion he tries to prove that judgment in art, in spite of the fact that it rests on the taste of the individual and, so far as immediate perception is concerned, does not get beyond the phenomenal world and its infinite otherwiseness, may nevertheless have universal validity.

Schiller, as is well known, took over from Kant the play theory, but eliminated from it, even more completely than he had done, the idea of purpose. The freedom of the imagination must not suffer any curtailment on teleological or other grounds. Everything, it is plain, in Schiller's view not only of art but of life hinges on his conception of freedom. One may grant Goethe that this conception underwent a progressive purification, yet one must insist that the freedom of the imagination as conceived by Schiller in his philosophical treatises and above all in his *Æsthetic Letters* remains predominantly expansive. No more essential question can be asked regarding any man than whether he regards liberty primarily as a taking on or as a throwing off of limitations; a question that is inextricably bound up with that of the 'infinite.' [1] It would be easy to multiply quotations to prove that Schiller associated the 'ideal' with the 'infinite' in the sense of the unbounded. In short one finds in Schiller the equivalent of the striving for endlessness (*Unendlichkeitstreben*) that

[1] I have discussed the 'infinite' in its relation to the romantic movement in *Rousseau and Romanticism*, pp. 250 ff.

pervades the whole German romantic movement
and to a lesser degree the romantic movement in
other countries. Once grant the romantic his notion
of the infinite as a *desirable* escape from limitations
and one might as well grant him everything. According to Aristotle and other Greeks, the infinite in
this sense is bad. It makes against an orderly and
proportionate view of life. Nietzsche, whose own
writings are very much infected with the 'striving
for endlessness,' can nevertheless on occasion speak
like a Greek of the whole tendency: '*Proportionate-
ness* is strange to us, let us confess it to ourselves;
our itching is really the itching for the infinite, the
immeasurable. Like the rider on his forward pant-
ing horse, we let the reins fall before the infinite, we
modern men, we semi-barbarians — and are only in
our highest bliss when we — *are in most danger.*' [1]
The danger to which Nietzsche refers and which the
Greek summed up in the word Nemesis is one to
which not merely the romanticist but occidental
man in general may be found to have exposed himself on a vast and perhaps unexampled scale by his
growing disregard of the law of measure.

[1] *Beyond Good and Evil*, translated by Helen Zimmern, pp. 169-70.

SCHILLER AS ÆSTHETIC THEORIST

The way in which one conceives of the liberty of
the imagination will be found to be closely connected
with the way in which one conceives of form. By
form I mean inner form, form in the human sense,
and not the mere outer form or technique that has
so often been offered in art and literature as a substitute for it. At its best, form in the human sense
may be defined as the imposition on the raw material of experience of some pattern that has been
apprehended with the aid of the imagination. In his
Dejection: an Ode Coleridge laments the loss of

> what nature gave me at my birth
> My shaping spirit of imagination.

Coleridge seems here to relate in romantic fashion
the 'shaping spirit' to the innate and spontaneous;
the 'shaping' that results in inner form is related
rather to imitation; the imagination is in the service
of the power in man that consciously and with reference to some sound model sets bounds to lawless
expansion.

The beauty that results from inner form has
sometimes been termed architectonic. It is felt as an
element of vital repose. By architectonic beauty
Schiller, on the other hand, does not mean beauty in

this specifically human sense nor indeed artistic beauty at all, but something organic — the excellence of form that the individual may owe to nature. In contrast to this natural beauty, the beauty of grace which he connects, not with repose, but with motion, appears to him more distinctively human. He seems here to be in line with the main modern tendency to associate beauty, whether in the individual or the work of art, with expression rather than with inner form, as I have been seeking to define it.[1] It is well to remember, however, that Schiller is far from being a clear and consistent writer. One source of difficulty is his wavering between the ethical (in the Kantian sense) and the æsthetic.[2] Inasmuch as he held that beauty has its source in nature and, in its more human aspect, is a feminine rather than a masculine prerogative, he would, as a Kantian, have been capable of apostrophizing it on occasion [3] in the words of Emerson:

[1] I have discussed the relative claims of form and expression in *The New Laokoon*, pp. 217 ff.

[2] Cf. Höffding, *History of Modern Philosophy*, II, 132. Schiller is Kantian in his praise of 'dignity,' Rousseauistic in his praise of the moral spontaneity of the 'beautiful soul.'

[3] See especially his essay *Über die Gefahr ästhetischer Sitten.*

SCHILLER AS ÆSTHETIC THEORIST

Thy dangerous glances
Make women of men;
New-born, we are melting
Into Nature again.

We have seen that, if the imagination is to play freely, it must, according to Schiller, be free from any purpose; for purpose means practically constraint and effort, whereas in the æsthetic state one enjoys a sort of ideal indolence. The Greeks, he says, 'freed the eternally blessed gods from the bonds of every aim, every duty and every care, and made idleness (*Müssiggang*) and indifference the envied lot of the divine estate: a purely human name for the freest and most exalted being.' An exaggerated echo of this passage is found in Friedrich Schlegel's celebrated *Elegy on Idleness* in *Lucinde*. Friedrich Schlegel also advances further along a path that Schiller opened by his ideas about the freedom of the imagination when he declares that 'the caprice of the poet suffers no law above itself.' Schiller was not himself a decadent æsthete,

[1] Schiller, like Kant, utters warnings against mere anarchy of the imagination (*Phantasterei*). One way of avoiding this anarchy is by art, which amounts practically to outer form or technique. One may, however, have a highly disciplined technique, even a classical technique, and combine it with an extreme vagrancy of the imagi-

but it is not difficult to cite passages from him which point in the direction of a decadent æstheticism.

That much creative art suggests a free play of the imagination of the kind Schiller describes no one would, I think, deny. The issue raised by the play theory is somewhat different. It appears perhaps most clearly in Schiller's assertion that 'man is entirely man only when he plays.' Reject this assertion and the whole edifice of Schiller's æsthetic theory crumbles at the base. Anyone who believes that the imagination needs to be disciplined to some human norm will reject it as a matter of first principles. He will maintain that one becomes 'entirely man' not by play but by work. By play, it may be replied, Schiller does not mean ordinary play. Neither does the humanist understand, by the exercise of ethical control over the imagination,

nation and sensibility. Precisely this combination is found in the prose of Anatole France.

Schiller, again (pp. 503–04), condemns those who fall into 'wild and fanciful effusions' as a result of having abandoned the real without attaining the ideal. When one examines what he means by the ideal, one finds that it involves an escape from, rather than an acceptance of, limitations. One must conclude that he offers no adequate criterion for distinguishing between a legitimate and an illegitimate play of the imagination.

[153]

ordinary work. Forget this distinction between play and work and one is menaced by a confusion of categories. One will presently be promoting art that has a place at most on the recreative side of life to the place that belongs only to art that is, in the Aristotelian sense, highly serious. For example, we are not to suppose that the travail of spirit with which Dante composed the *Divine Comedy* and which, as he tells us, made him lean for many years, had to do merely with the technique or outer form of his poem; it had to do even more with its inner form, its human and religious substance. Schiller himself was the last person to assign to art and literature a purely recreative rôle. He has in particular uttered a protest against the attitude that we associate nowadays with the tired business man. He is one of the first indeed to employ the actual phrase (*den erschöpften Geschäftsmann*). Yet nothing is more certain than that the play theory favors the tired business man and in general the utilitarian who, having put forth his effort in an entirely different direction, turns to art and literature for the refreshment and solace of his idle moments. It is no accident that the best known

partisan of the play theory in English is the utilitarian Herbert Spencer. Nay, the whole point of
view is already in germ in the prophet of the utilitarian movement, Francis Bacon. 'The use of this
feigned history [i.e., poetry],' he says, 'hath been to
give some show of satisfaction to the mind of man
in those points wherein the nature of things doth
deny it... it doth raise and erect the mind, by
submitting the shows of things to the desires of the
mind, whereas reason doth bow and buckle the mind
unto the nature of things.' The scientific observer,
in short, is to submit to the discipline of reality,
whereas the poet may shatter this sorry scheme of
things and then remould it nearer to the heart's
desire, may, in short, let his imagination play
freely. It is plain, at all events, that the artist whose
imagination is ideally 'free' in the sense Schiller has
defined in his *Æsthetic Letters* does not achieve the
reality at which the man of science aims when he
bows and buckles his reason to the nature of things.
There is, indeed, Schiller would have us believe, an
incompatibility between reason, on the one hand,
and imagination and the æsthetic attitude on the
other. 'In æsthetic judgments,' says Schiller, 'our

[155]

interest is not in morality for itself but only in freedom, and morality can please our imagination only in so far as it makes freedom visible. Hence there is a manifest confusion of boundaries when one demands moral purpose in æsthetic things and, in order to widen the realm of reason, seeks to force the imagination out of its proper domain. Imagination will either have to be subjected entirely to reason and in that case all æsthetic effect is lost, or reason will have to yield a part of its sovereignty to imagination, and in that case there is no great gain for morality. As a result of pursuing two different ends, you will run the risk of missing both. You will chain the freedom of phantasy through moral restrictions, and disturb the necessity of reason through the caprice (*Willkühr*) of imagination.' [1]

Evidently anyone who aspires to be a perfect æsthete must be prepared to make sacrifices. He must turn his back on reason, on ethical purpose and on reality in any possible sense, one might suppose, of that elusive term. Beauty, as Schiller conceives it, is pure appearance (*Schein*) without substance —

[1] Page 176.

a realm of shadows. It is above all an escape from
the actual:

> Fliehet aus dem engen dumpfen Leben
> In der Schönheit Schattenreich.[1]

As the romantic imagination soars into its own
'intense inane'

> des Erdenlebens
> Schweres Traumbild sinkt und sinkt und sinkt.

It is not easy to distinguish between the 'realm
of shadows' into which Schiller would have us
retreat and the *pays des chimères* that solicits the
imagination of Rousseau or the 'ivory tower' of the
later romanticists. If this is the 'ideal,' as Schiller
assures us it is, it is not easy to distinguish between
the ideal and mere illusion. To be sure, by way of
compensation for his sacrifice of reason, purpose
and reality, the æsthete may, according to Schiller,
hope to enjoy the highest good. By taking refuge
in the region opened up to him by the free play of

---

[1] *Das Reich der Schatten.* This poem (also entitled *Das Reich der Formen* and *Das Ideal und das Leben*) is closely related in theme to the *Aesthetische Briefe.* One can only admire the success with which Schiller has in *Das Reich der Schatten* transmuted difficult philosophical abstractions into genuine poetry. At the same time one must insist that the beauty of art of the first order is not of this 'escape' variety. Its form is rich in content; it is not, like Schiller's 'form,' all outside without inside, a mere hollow semblance.

his imagination he is no longer subject to the necessity of the natural order nor again to that of the moral order (as conceived by Kant); above all he no longer suffers from the conflict between the two orders.

How far is Schiller's scheme for dealing with the inner conflict of which man is conscious, primitivistic? In other words, does he hope that man may escape from his present disharmony by a recovery of the unity of instinct that he is supposed to have possessed before his fall from 'nature'? In replying to this question we shall need to turn from the *Æsthetic Letters* and the essay on *Grace and Dignity* to the treatise that was, according to Goethe, immediately responsible for the rise of a romantic school — that, namely, on *Simple and Sentimental Poetry*.

I have already pointed out the relationship between Schiller's praise of the 'blessed gods' and Friedrich Schlegel's *Elegy on Idleness*. Schlegel asserts in the Elegy that 'the more divine man is, the more fully does he resemble the plant.' One is reminded of a couplet of Schiller's written fairly late in life (1795) in which he affirms that what the

SCHILLER AS ÆSTHETIC THEORIST

plant is unconsciously, that one should consciously seek to become.[1] It must be granted that in the treatise on *Simple and Sentimental Poetry* he strikes a somewhat different note. The treatise opens, to be sure, with the glorification of the child and of the man of genius who retains the childlike virtues. Schiller proceeds to raise the question, however, whether one's longing for 'simple nature does not arise from one's indolence rather than from one's wounded moral sense that longs for its harmony.' He finally decides that 'the goal towards which man strives through culture (*Kultur*) is infinitely to be preferred to the goal to which he attains through nature.'[2] This, says Professor Lovejoy, is Schiller's epoch-making conclusion; it marks perhaps the most decisive single turning-point in the history of the whole romantic movement. In order to make good his contention, Professor Lovejoy would have to prove that Schiller has in this treatise broken radically with primitivism. Before deciding this

[1] Suchst du das Höchste, das Grösste? Die Pflanze kann es dich lehren.
   Was sie willenlos ist, sey du es wollend — das ists!
[2] Page 453. The Goedeke edition has *Kultur* instead of *Natur*, a misprint that makes the sentence meaningless.

question, one must evidently be clear as to one's definition of primitivism. Up to a certain point there is little room for disagreement: the primitivist seeks to return to a nature that is conceived to be simple or naïve in contrast with the sophistication of an advanced civilization. But how simple does one's nature need to be if one is to be accounted a primitivist? Professor Lovejoy has developed elsewhere the extraordinary thesis that Rousseau is not primitivistic in his *Discourse on the Origins of Inequality*; one of his chief arguments for this thesis is that Rousseau prefers the pastoral stage of human development to sheer savagery. On the contrary, this preference of Rousseau's may be taken as convincing proof that he is a primitivist. One cannot repeat too often that the 'nature' to which the primitivist seeks to return does not correspond to anything real but is a projection of the idyllic or pastoral imagination. Nature in the idyllic sense is as devoid of substance as the 'shadow-realm of beauty' into which Schiller would have us flee, and is indeed psychologically closely related to it. Schiller says that 'he too was born in Arcadia.' The question I would raise is whether, so far as the

ultimate quality of his imagination is concerned, he
ever got out of Arcadia. As to his theory of the
imagination, it seems to me that no doubt is
possible. He not only proclaims the idyll the highest
form of art, but the Elysium to which he would
have us press forward is, like Rousseau's state of
nature, plainly idyllic. How then about his attack
on the indolence of the Rousseauistic primitivist, his
preference for culture over 'nature'? One must
admit that in his attitude towards the intellect, at
least, Schiller is not primitivistic. He is not ready
to say with Rousseau himself and various Rous-
seauists that 'the man who thinks is a depraved
animal.' If the German romantics were as a rule
not inclined to disparage the intellect and the type
of 'culture' one may owe to it, the credit is possibly
due in part to Schiller. In deciding, however, how
far anyone is a primitivist the important point to
determine is not his attitude towards the intellect,
but whether as a result of following the lure of the
idyllic imagination he has been led to set up
emotional expansion as a substitute for a concentration of the ethical will. The indolence that consists
in a failure to exercise control over the imagination

and emotions is something far subtler than the indolence against which Schiller utters his warning. If one yields to this form of indolence, one may, like many of the German romantics, develop a refined culture (in Schiller's sense) and at the same time fail to establish a harmony between this culture and one's imaginative and emotional life. Rousseau spoke once for all for this class of persons when he said that his 'heart and head did not seem to belong to the same individual.' The contrast and conflict between the 'conscious' and the 'unconscious' of which one hears so much in the modern movement has a similar origin.

In dealing with this problem of the divided self, Schiller is, then, in large measure primitivistic even in the treatise on *Simple and Sentimental Poetry.* He applies the epithet simple or naïve, it will be remembered, to the individual or the group still at one with 'nature.' The epithet sentimental he applies to the individual who looks back longingly from his sophistication to this lost unity. 'It was certainly a very different feeling,' he says, 'that filled the soul of Homer when he depicted his 'divine cowherd' giving hospitality to Ulysses,

[162]

from that which agitated the soul of young Werther
when he read the *Odyssey* on issuing from a polite
gathering in which he had found only boredom.'[1] If
one keeps in mind that what Schiller calls 'nature'
is largely nostalgia, the difficulties into which he has
got himself involved by this primitivistic opposition
should be apparent. He is comparing a sentimental
attitude that actually did exist, of which indeed he
had abundant personal experience, with a natural
state that is for the most part a dream. Somewhat
similar to Schiller's is the contrast established by
Herder and others between a *Naturpoesie* which is
spontaneous, which may indeed be the collective
emanation of a whole folk, and a *Kunstpoesie*
which no longer wells up from the depths of the
unconscious and is therefore forced to be painfully
imitative. This whole contrast is rapidly growing
obsolete.

Æsthetic theorizing, one might suppose, has value
only in so far as it is of aid in forming sound concrete
judgments. Anyone who has threaded his way
through the extraordinarily intricate labyrinth of
æsthetic theorizing that extends from Kant and the

[1] Page 445.

SCHILLER AS ÆSTHETIC THEORIST

English predecessors of Kant through Schiller to the Schlegels and beyond must conclude that this theorizing, so far from having been of aid in the formation of taste, has been rather a source of error. One should not indeed venture upon such an assertion without the proper qualifications. Schiller, for example, speaks very much to the purpose of the conflict between the 'ideal' and the 'real' as depicted by certain sentimental writers like the Goethe of *Werther*. Rousseau, says Schiller again, either seeks nature or else avenges her by art.[1] This is excellent, provided that by 'nature' one understands Rousseau's idyllic imaginings and by his avenging nature his attacks on Parisian sophistication. It is when Schiller seeks representatives of the two attitudes — the simple and the sentimental — in the poets and periods of the past that he goes most palpably astray. He makes of the urbane Horace, for example, the founder of the sentimental school 'of which he remains the unsurpassed model.'[2] In labeling Homer (along with Bodmer!) a naïve poet, he is still more unlucky. His most remarkable

[1] Page 467.
[2] Pages 445–46.

aberration, however, is to have looked not merely upon this or that Greek but upon the Greeks in general as naïve! Schiller ridiculed the 'Græco-mania' of Friedrich Schlegel in his early phase. Yet he is himself an authentic ancestor of what may be termed romantic Hellenism — one of the most singular products of the opposition established by the primitivist between the spontaneous and the imitative. The Greeks as Schiller pictures them are at once children of nature in Rousseau's sense and perfect æsthetes in his own sense. The kinship between the two dreams is not surprising, seeing that they both proceed from the same quality of imagination. Emerson is close to Schiller when he affirms in his essay on *History* that the Greeks carved perfect statues simply because they were unusually healthy children. 'The Greeks,' he says, 'are not reflective. ... They combine the energy of manhood with the engaging unconsciousness of childhood. Our reverence for them is our reverence for childhood.' It is scarcely necessary to remark that there has been a bountiful supply at all times of healthy children and of manhood that has remained adolescent and even infantile, but no repetition of the 'Greek miracle.'

SCHILLER AS ÆSTHETIC THEORIST

I am not maintaining of course, that Schiller's portrayal of the Greeks, not only in his prose but in a poem like the *Gods of Greece*, is entirely false, but merely that he has in no small measure baptized with the name of Greece his own nostalgia. It is in part due to Schiller that the Greek spirit itself has become, in Walter Pater's phrase, the 'sangrail of an endless pilgrimage.' This particular nostalgia might even be pushed to the point of madness as we see in Hölderlin,[1] who was under the influence of both Rousseau and Schiller.

The simple poet who is at one with himself and nature would seem to have an advantage over the sentimental poet who suffers from an inner disharmony. One finds, however, prefigured in Schiller the revulsion of feeling that overtakes Renan in the midst of his *Prayer on the Acropolis* — one of the most perfect bits of romantic Hellenism in the modern movement. After having glorified Athene and the Greeks, Renan dismisses them as the 'apostles of ennui.' They were perfect because they accepted limitations. Athene's brow would

[1] Mich verlangt ins ferne Land hinüber
Nach Alcäus und Anakreon, etc.

not be so calm if her head embraced 'diverse kinds of beauty.' To this narrowness Renan opposes a sheer expansion of wonder and curiosity. In somewhat the same fashion Schiller argues that, though the sentimental poet longs to be a Greek, the Greek himself did not long; and this lack of aspiration must be regarded as a weakness. At the same time simplicity is in itself something very precious. One should strive to combine the simple with the sentimental: 'For the idea of a beautiful humanity is not exhausted by either, but can only issue from the union of both.' [1]

Some such reasoning as this must have been in the mind of Friedrich Schlegel when he deserted the Greeks for the mediævals and those moderns who seemed to him to have retained the mediæval virtues. The men of the middle ages were still capable of the unity of feeling that belongs only to the simple, and had at the same time a sense of the infinite. Those who are in the mediæval Christian tradition are not satisfied, like the Greeks, as A. W. Schlegel was to put it later, with the enjoyment of the present moment, but hover between recollection and hope.

[1] Page 509.

SCHILLER AS ÆSTHETIC THEORIST

It is not easy to determine the exact extent of Schiller's influence on the Schlegels. Nothing is in general more uncertain and elusive than these questions of influence when followed up in detail. One may, however, affirm that Friedrich Schlegel developed Schiller's opposition between the simple and the sentimental (with certain important modifications) into that between the classic and the romantic. Certain ambiguities in these terms that persist even to the present day can be traced not only to the fact that the founder of the original romantic school had a genius for confusion, but that, at the time of making his doctrinal distinctions, he was in an unusually vacillating mood even for him. In November, 1797, Friedrich wrote to his brother Wilhelm: 'I cannot conveniently send you my elucidation of the word romantic because — it is a hundred and twenty-five pages long!' Wilhelm, who popularized the ideas of his brother, so far from clarifying them, tended rather to add confusions of his own. With the aid of Madame de Staël the confused contrast between the classical, on the one hand, and the mediæval or the romantic, on the other, rapidly gained European currency. The chapters of the book on Germany,[1] in which she elaborates this contrast, probably contain as much confusion as any similar amount of writing in literature. When she invites us to turn from the mechanical imitation of classical antiquity, as exemplified in Boileau and other writers of the French seventeenth century, to what is for us indigenous, namely, chivalry and mediæval Christianity, she is doubly misleading. At their best the men of the French seventeenth century and of the middle ages were both imitative, not in a mechanical but in a vital way. Moreover, the models that they imitated, though with very different emphasis, were supplied by the same traditions. In general one may say in reply to the German primitivists whom Madame de Staël so largely echoes, that though there may have been nostalgia in the middle ages and the sense of the 'infinite' that goes with it, this nostalgia is not to be identified with the religious aspiration of the period; nor did the cohesion of mediæval society derive primarily from feeling: so far as the mediæval achieved outer unity, it was due to the fact that he was part of a hierarchy that had

[1] Especially IIᵉ Partie, ch. XI.

its ultimate sanction in the divine will; so far as he achieved inner unity, it was due to a similar subordination of the lower to the higher — to all that is summed up in the word humility.

Schiller's æsthetic theory was influential not merely on the Schlegels but on Novalis, Schelling, Hegel, Schopenhauer, and others. This theory is of course only one tributary in a vast stream of tendency. It is often difficult to distinguish Schiller's contribution to the stream from that of others. One may say, however, that the very boldness with which he equates the idyllic quality of imagination with the ideal is important for the whole modern period. There has been built up during this period a vast structure of 'idealism' that has this quality of imagination — what the psycho-analysts call the 'escape' quality — at its base. It is this element of escape that links the exaltation of the idyll in the essay on *Simple and Sentimental Poetry*, with the 'shadow-realm' of pure beauty that Schiller celebrates in the *Æsthetic Letters* and elsewhere. He thus encourages a divorce of art from life and is indeed one of the ancestors of the doctrine of art for art's sake.[1]

[1] 'The opposition between art and life posited by Kant and

SCHILLER AS ÆSTHETIC THEORIST

Many of those who professed to repudiate this doctrine were preparing its triumph by the hollowness of the ends they would have art serve. 'Art for art's sake may be beautiful,' says Hugo, 'but art for progress is still more beautiful.' When we come to examine Hugo's idea of progress we find that it is itself only an idyllic dream — not unrelated to Schiller's Elysium; a dream that does not, like a true purpose, impose any effective discipline upon the imagination. It is possible indeed to be a perfect 'idealist' of the humanitarian type and at the same time live, like Hugo himself, in a state of extreme imaginative unrestraint. 'Let us not forget it,' says Scherer, 'the masses are idealistic; they refuse to recognize the most thoroughly established facts when they are the victims of them.' One may have sympathy with the masses when they take refuge from certain facts in idyllic imaginings, even though they thus expose themselves to a head-on collision with

Schiller was ridden to death by Schopenhauer,' says Höffding (*History of Modern Philosophy*, II, p. 234). Like many other 'escapists' Schopenhauer gave the first place among the arts to music.

The earliest known instance of the phrase *l'art pour l'art* is found in Benjamin Constant's *Journal* (10 Feb., 1804; not published until 1895). As appears from the context, he coined the phrase with direct reference to the æsthetic theories of the Germans — especially Kant and Schiller.

the Nature of Things. But when a man sets up as a major prophet like Hugo with no other equipment than 'ideals' that have their source in similar imaginings, it is not so easy to be indulgent.

On the inevitable collapse of ideals of this kind the artist who has shared them may reason that, inasmuch as his attempt to consecrate his art to some adequate end has proved illusory, he will henceforth regard this art as an end in itself. The doctrine of *l'art pour l'art* professed by a Baudelaire or a Leconte de Lisle, for example, stands in fairly close relationship to the revolutionary fiasco of 1848. However one may account for this doctrine historically, the practical upshot of it has been a failure to find any middle term between mere moralism and æsthetic irresponsibility. This failure is only one aspect of the failure of the modern age in general to find any ethical center on which its partial aims and activities finally converge. We are inclined to smile at the assertion of the late Stuart Sherman that 'Beauty has a heart full of service.' It is well to remember, however, that the idea of service is not necessarily rotarian. Goethe himself said that the Muse is a good accompanist but a poor leader.

SCHILLER AS ÆSTHETIC THEORIST

If one asks what the Muse is to accompany, one may be forced to conclude that a good deal has been lost in our modern world with the decline of the idea of divine service. The equivalent of this form of service — the idea that art should look beyond itself — can be found of course in other faiths and philosophies of life besides Christianity, even in a non-theistic faith like Buddhism. Art that is not in the service of the supersensuous is likely to become, not an end in itself, but a mere servant of the senses. There is at least this much to be said for the obscurantist view of art that can be traced in the Occident from the early Christian centuries and in certain respects from Plato himself.[1]

A word seems to be called for in this context on the use of the epithet 'pure.' This epithet, as applied to various modern activities, has come to be a

---

[1] Art for art's sake is hardly as sinister, however, as Tennyson would have us believe in the following lines, though some might maintain that even this extreme attitude has been justified by much recent practice:

> Art for Art's sake! Hail, truest Lord of Hell!
>   Hail, Genius, Master of the Moral Will!
> 'The filthiest of all paintings painted well
>   Is mightier than the purest painted ill!'
> Yes, mightier than the purest painted well,
> So prone are we toward the broad way to Hell!

way of proclaiming that these activities are self-sufficient. Thus we have not merely pure art and pure poetry, but pure history, pure science, etc. According to Croce, for example, history ceases to be pure, if the historian ventures on moral judgments; if he asserts, let us say, that Lincoln was a better man than Nero. If Professor Compton or another succeeds in releasing the stores of energy that are supposed to be locked up in the atom, we may be sure that he will feel immaculate, whatever the practical consequences of his discovery, even though men use it to blow themselves off the planet; for he is a servant of *pure* science. It goes without saying that poetry has undergone a formidable purgation in the interests of its purity. Baudelaire praises as the type of the pure artist the essentially empty Gautier: he never establishes any irrelevant relationship between the beautiful and the true or the good. According to Abbé Bremond, poetry becomes pure in direct proportion, one is tempted to say, as it loses human substance. When at its purest it is little more apparently than sound without sense.[1]

The cult of purity, it should be observed, is some-

[1] Cf. p. 124.

thing entirely distinct from that of the clear-cut type
(*genre tranché*). On the contrary, the poets who
have been praised for their purity are the very ones
who were busy in blurring the boundaries between
poetry and the other arts — Gautier, for example,
between poetry and painting, Baudelaire (in certain
of his poems) and some of the symbolists, between
poetry and music, etc. This breaking down of
frontiers may be shown to be dubious even from the
point of view of technique or outer form; it is even
more dubious from the point of view of inner form
which requires imaginative allegiance to some central norm or scale of values set above any particular art.

One may properly inquire indeed whether *pure*
beauty, beauty divorced from the total symmetry
of life and pursued *in vacuo*, is not, as Flaubert himself, an ardent devotee of *l'art pour l'art*, exclaimed
on one occasion, a phantom. A survey of the whole
movement from the eighteenth century down will, I
think, result in a growing distrust of persons who
take refuge in a cult of Beauty (with a capital B) as
well as of philosophers who seek to define Beauty in
this abstract and general sense. In spite of the

æsthetes and most æstheticians, one is justified in affirming that there are various kinds of beauty which differ from one another not merely in degree but in kind. One cannot grant Baudelaire that the only alternative to accepting his idea of Beauty is to be a Puritan or a philistine. 'A lowering cloud,' he complains, 'come from Geneva, Boston or hell, has intercepted the fair rays of the sun of æsthetics.' One may note in passing that a descendant of the Puritans, living in the immediate neighborhood of Boston, struck out a more fortunate phrase for Baudelaire's attitude than any he himself succeeded in coining: 'Beauty is its own excuse for being.' One should recollect that, though Emerson held apparently that his phrase had universal validity, he actually applied it to a special type of beauty — that of the 'Rhodora in the woods.' The notion of beauty as an end in itself and the æsthetic attitude in general have been much advanced — and that from the time of Addison's papers on the imagination in the *Spectator* — by the growing appreciation of outer nature, especially wild nature. One should surely not be indifferent to beauty of this type, much less assume an ascetic attitude towards it, after the fashion of the Jansenists, of whom it has been said that they disparaged unduly the miracle of the creation in their desire to exalt the miracle of the redemption. One may even admit a purposeful element in nature, though one do not go so far as to proclaim with the psalmist: 'The heavens declare the glory of God; and the firmament sheweth his handiwork.' At the same time it is well to remember that nature's ways are not man's ways and that the purpose that appears in her processes has little relation to the purpose that appears in some distinctively human creation. Perhaps the most widely accepted idea about beauty is that it arises from the achievement of unity in variety. One falls into confusion if one supposes that this idea, sound enough in itself, is exemplified in the same way in wild nature as it is when man consciously imposes order on what were else chaotic. The beauty of the 'Rhodora in the woods' differs, not merely in degree, but in kind from that of the Parthenon. A Greek of the great period would have listened sympathetically, one may suppose, to Keats when he complained that the poetasters of the eighteenth century had fallen into a wretched formalism in spite of the fact that 'Beauty

was awake.' It is probable, however, that he would
have been a bit disconcerted when he learned what
Keats meant by Beauty:

> The winds of heaven blew, the ocean roll'd
> Its gathering waves, etc.

If we omit the capital B so dear to the æsthete and
ask how beauty, as Keats conceived it, differs from
beauty as a Greek normally conceived it, we are
brought back to the problem of inner form. Inner
form, I have said, requires the conscious imitation
of a model built up from certain constant factors in
human experience. Beauty that is thus based on the
acceptance of a universal is no longer irresponsible,
no longer the result of free imaginative play in
Schiller's sense. It can no longer be estimated in itself but only with reference to the rightness of the
idea of the universal that it serves and to its success
in rendering this idea. The æsthete who sets up a
cult of pure Beauty and the æsthetician who hopes
to define Beauty *per se* would both seem to be
caught in a hopeless dilemma. If one makes of
beauty a matter of feeling, as the very word æsthetic
implies, one rests it on something that is per-
petually changing, not only from man to man but in

the same man; a beauty that is thus relativistic and impressionistic finally becomes meaningless. If, on the other hand, one affirms a universal element in beauty one is brought back from æsthetics and its claims to set up as an independent subject, to general philosophy. Roughly speaking, one's notions of beauty will tend to vary according as one's total attitude towards life is naturalistic, humanistic or religious.

In dealing with the problems of technique or outer form the æsthetician may of course have much to say that is relevant. There is even a certain place here for the despised rules — above all, perhaps, rules what to avoid. It is hard to see, however, that the æsthetician is justified merely on this score in setting up his subject as something distinct from ordinary criticism. When one passes from outer to inner form one enters into a region of imponderables that eludes both rules and scientific measurement; a region that is sometimes summed up in the word 'soul.' This word has tended to change its meaning with the drift away from the traditional unifications of life towards the unique and the expressive. As employed by a typical modernist like Anatole

France, for example, 'soul' is synonymous with a shifting sensibility.

How, it may be asked, may one recognize the presence of inner form? One is forced to fall back on Dr. Johnson's phrase 'the grandeur of generality.' This phrase reminds one again of the admirable treatise *On the Sublime* attributed to Longinus. The mark of great literature, according to Longinus, is a certain elevation. The test of the genuineness of this elevation and distinction in any particular literary work is its long-continued and universal appeal. Like other key-words, the epithet sublime underwent a strange transformation in the eighteenth century. If anyone inclines to identify change with progress let him begin by comparing the treatise of Longinus with Burke's *Inquiry into the Sublime and Beautiful*; [1] and then let him trace the theory and practice of sublimity from Burke to Victor Hugo [2] and beyond. In the case of speculations on the sub-

[1] The *Inquiry* was published in 1756 when Burke was only twenty-seven. One wonders whether in later life he did not look back upon it as a youthful indiscretion.

[2] Professor W. F. Giese speaks of 'Hugo's taste for whatever is wild and terrible and his disdain for what is simply beautiful.' This taste of Hugo's reveals the influence, though no doubt the indirect influence, of Burke.

lime as in the case of kindred speculations on the beautiful, one needs to follow the line of development that leads from Burke to Kant and from Kant to Schiller. It must be said, however, that the ideas set forth by Schiller in his essay on the Sublime are less important for the modern movement than certain other ideas found in his æsthetic treatises — especially the idea that one may become 'free' and truly human simply by 'playing.' In view of the importance of the subject — for many of the great romantics aimed at sublimity even more than at beauty — I am going to discuss it somewhat more fully than would be justified, on the scale of the present essay, by Schiller's treatment of it.

Let us begin by reminding ourselves that Longinus does not make any distinction between the sublime and the beautiful. Great literature, he says in substance, must satisfy two requirements: it must have inner elevation and formal excellence; in dealing with this latter requirement he enters into minute discussions of literary technique. The first requirement he sums up in the phrase: 'Sublimity is the echo of a great soul.' Soul in the Longinian sense (closely allied to the Platonic meaning) is not primarily emotional nor again intellectual. It is something of which one has the immediate 'sentiment' or perception in another, in virtue of a kindred quality of soul in oneself. La Bruyère is purely Longinian when he writes: 'When what you read elevates your spirit and inspires in you noble and courageous sentiments do not seek any other rule for judging the work: it is good and made by a master hand.' La Bruyère is also Longinian when he insists on the importance of *métier* or technique.[1] In short, like Longinus, he does justice to both inner and outer form.

What tends to suffer in the contrast established by Burke between the sublime and the beautiful is the Longinian quality of 'soul.' It is not easy to combine loftiness of spirit with the sensationalism on which Burke bases his main position. The beautiful he identifies with the small, the smooth, the agreeable, etc.; the sublime with the vast, the vague, the obscure, the terrible, the painful, etc. — all ideas that are absent from Longinus with the exception perhaps of vastness in the passage in which he admits an element of sublimity in certain spectacles of nature (Ch. XXXV).

[1] Cf. p. 220.

SCHILLER AS ÆSTHETIC THEORIST

Kant is less sensationalistic and psychological than Burke and at the same time more metaphysical. He is also much more concerned than Burke with the relation of the sublime to the moral law. Kant's moral sublimity would seem to suffer from the defects of his practical reason, which as I have already said, assumes a supersensuous realm, but gives one no direct access to it. 'The expression of the sublime often needs the spur,' says Longinus, 'but it is also true that it often needs the curb.' This curb, if it is not to be merely formalistic, would seem to call for some degree of supersensuous perception. At all events one hears nothing of the need of a curb in Kant's discussion of sublimity, nor again in that of Schiller. Schiller, one may note in passing, retains in his idea of the sublime the element of painfulness that had been introduced into it by Burke. He associates it like Kant not only with wild nature, but wild nature, it may be, in its disorderly aspects.[1]

Unless one recognizes that the sublime requires a

---

[1] Strictly speaking for both Kant and Schiller sublimity is not in nature itself, but in him who beholds it. We are reminded of Pascal's conception of man as the *roseau pensant*. His possession of mind makes him superior to the forces of the outer world, however vast and terrible.

curb or *frein vital*, it is hard to see how it is possible to protect inner form against the romantic craving for the unlimited and immeasurable. The way is open for the Titanism of a Hugo, for his praise, for example, of the genius who is 'badly bridled on purpose by God in order that he may soar with free sweep of the wing through the infinite.' For Hugo the sublime is a sort of mixture of imaginative unrestraint and sheer emotional vehemence. It is not easy to discover in this mixture the transcendent element that is, according to Longinus (Ch. XXXVI), required in the true sublime. According to certain romantics, indeed, one may hope to become sublime, not by rising above, but by sinking below the rational level. Alfred de Vigny, for example, would have us pattern ourselves on the '*sublime* animals.' The epithet probably reached its lowest depth even in romantic usage, when Baudelaire applied it to the virgins of Lesbos for reasons one prefers not to mention.[1]

[1] Vierges au cœur *sublime*, honneur de l'Archipel,
Votre religion comme une autre est auguste,
Votre amour se rira de l'enfer et du ciel!
Que nous veulent les lois du juste et de l'injuste?

For Rousseau's use of the epithet see p. 18; for Wordsworth's, see p. 53.

SCHILLER AS ÆSTHETIC THEORIST

It is plain that we cannot look to the romantic sublime for an effective counterpoise to what has been termed man's innate penchant for the bathos. According to Longinus the two chief enemies of the sublime are love of money and love of pleasure — proclivities that were never more dominant than they are today. I have the impression indeed (I hope a mistaken one) that our own time suffers in an almost unexampled degree from lack of elevation. As it explores depth on depth of triviality, it seems in a fair way to achieve at least one kind of infinitude — the kind, namely, to which Swift refers in speaking of the poets of his day:

> — the height we know;
> *'Tis only infinite below.*

I am, however, digressing from Schiller, who is only remotely responsible, if at all, for the proficiency we have attained in the 'art of sinking.' Furthermore, whatever one may think of Schiller as an æsthetician, one must recognize in the man himself an essential nobility of spirit. This is praise that it is scarcely possible to accord to the Schlegels and others who came under his influence. His æsthetic treatises have admirable details. Nevertheless one's total estimate of these treatises, if my own analysis is correct, must be unfavorable: he sought primitivistic solutions of problems that can only be solved aright on humanistic or even religious lines, and in so doing got himself involved in intellectual and emotional sophistry.

VI

JULIEN BENDA

THE present moment in French literature would seem to be unusually confused. As a first step in getting one's bearings in a somewhat chaotic situation, one may perhaps distinguish between the writers who are still in the main modern movement and those who are in more or less marked opposition to it. This movement has been in one of its most important aspects primitivistic. Rousseau, with his tendency to disparage intellect in favor of the unconscious felicities of instinct, is, though not the first, easily the most influential of the primitivists.

Among the more prominent living opponents of primitivism one may mention M. Ernest Seillière, who has been developing in numerous volumes the thesis that Rousseau's doctrine of man's natural goodness, in theory fraternal, results practically in an 'irrational imperialism'; likewise M. Charles Maurras and the group of *l'Action française*, who, seeing in Rousseauism an alien intrusion into the French tradition, seek to restore this tradition, classical, Catholic and monarchial, such as it existed, for example, in the Age of Louis XIV. The members of this group, it is important to note, are less interested in classicism and religion for their own sake than as necessary supports for what they term an 'integral nationalism.' There is again the neo-scholastic group of which M. Jacques Maritain is probably the most gifted member. This group parts company with the modern movement not merely from the eighteenth century but from the Renaissance. In his *Three Reformers* M. Maritain assails Luther and Descartes as well as Rousseau, finding no firm anchorage for the spirit short of the *Summa* of Saint Thomas Aquinas.

Finally M. Julien Benda is one of the most interesting of those who oppose, on various grounds, the modern movement. He is an isolated figure in the contemporary battle of ideas in France. Some might even say that he pushes his independence to a point that is slightly quixotic. He has taken issue not only with the modernists but with many of the enemies of modernism. He discovers, for instance, a temper unduly narrow and exclusive in the neo-scholastics, a proneness to look on themselves alone as true men and on all others, who are outside the circle of their orthodoxy, as 'dogs and swine.' He detects again romantic elements in the cult that M. Maurras renders to reason, and is unable to see that 'integral nationalism' of the type promoted by *l'Action française* is genuinely Catholic or classical. Rousseau would, as a matter of fact, have the right to say (in the words of Emerson's Brahma) of many of those who profess to be reacting from him: 'When me they fly, I am the wings.'

M. Benda has been concerned primarily, not with the older forms of the primitivistic movement, but with those it has assumed during the last thirty or forty years. He has been above all an implacable enemy of the form it has taken in the philosophy of Bergson, of the anti-intellectual trend of this philosophy and its tendency to present as a spiritual illumination what is at bottom only the latest refinement of Rousseauistic revery. As a sample of revery thus setting up as a 'mystic union with the essence of things' M. Benda cites the following passage from M. Edouard LeRoy, Bergson's disciple and successor at the Collège de France: 'Distinctions have disappeared. Words no longer have any value. One hears welling forth mysteriously the sources of consciousness, like an unseen trickling of living water through the darkness of a moss-grown grotto. I am dissolved in the joy of becoming. I give myself over to the delight of being an ever streaming reality. I no longer know whether I see perfumes, or breathe sounds or taste colors,' [1] etc.

The point of view is related to that of the contemporary French group known as the *surréalistes* who hope to achieve creative spontaneity by diving into the depths of the subrational. The *surréalistes* in turn have much in common with the English and American writers who abandon themselves to the 'stream of consciousness.'

M. Benda has studied above all the ravages of Bergsonism in the polite circles of French society — the circles whose traditional rôle it has been to maintain the principle of leisure. The influence of women has always been marked in these circles — but with a difference. In the older French society there were still men of leisure who set the tone and

[1] This sort of revery is of course closely related to the confusion of the arts with which I have sought to deal in *The New Laokoon*.

to whom the women deferred. In an industrial society like our own, on the other hand, the men are taken up more and more with business and money-making. In the meanwhile the women have been encouraged in the belief that they are richer than men in the type of intuition that Bergson exalts above reason. Hence their growing contempt for the masculine point of view. Men themselves are inclined to grant them, at least in art and literature, this superiority.

It would not be difficult to find an American parallel to M. Benda's picture in *Belphégor* of the great industrialist who bows down before his wife's superiority because she gets up at noon and plays a little Schumann on the piano. Men are even more absorbed in utilitarian pursuits in America than in France, and even more inclined to turn over to women the cultural values which have been a chief concern of the great civilizations of the past.

Belphégor, though it continues M. Benda's previous onslaughts on Bergsonism, has a somewhat wider scope. The tendency to grant the primacy to emotion that this work assails goes at least as far back as the sentimentalists of the eighteenth cen-

tury. When Faust, for example, exclaims that
'feeling is all,' he sums up Rousseau in his essential
aspect, on the one hand, and, on the other, looks
forward to 'the greedy thirst for immediacy' that is
the theme of *Belphégor*. One may grant at most
that this thirst has led in the case of certain contemporaries to a more complete sloughing off of the
traditional disciplines than one usually finds in the
earlier primitivists. The net result from the outset
of the quest of sensation and emotional intensity for
their own sake, has been, in Mr. Santayana's phrase,
a 'red-hot irrationality.'

Himself a Jew, M. Benda attributes the decadence he describes in part to Jewish influence; but
there have always been, he goes on to explain, two
types of Jews — those who in ancient times worshiped Belphegor[1] and those who worshiped Je-
hovah. As a modern example of the former type, he
mentions Bergson; of the latter, Spinoza. Moreover, the Jew would not have been able to act thus
deleteriously on the Gentile if the power of psychic

---

[1] The name of this divinity appears in the Septuagint as Beel-
phegor and in the King James Version as Baal-peor. It has been
inferred, especially from Numbers, chapter 25, that the cult rendered to Baal-peor was licentious.

resistance of the Gentile had not been seriously lowered. One reason for this lowered resistance, M. Benda surmises, has been the decline of classical study. It might be supposed in that case that one way to fortify the cultivated classes against an irrational surrender to their emotions would be a more humanistic type of education. But M. Benda has no hope of a return to the humanities. He anticipates a future even worse than the present — a sort of indefinite progression in unreason.

It may be, however, that M. Benda is unduly gloomy in his forebodings, that even this tree will not quite grow to heaven. It is an encouraging sign that the rightness of his analysis of the emotional excess has been widely recognized — so much so that the term 'Belphegorism' has entered into current French usage. One may profit by M. Benda's analysis without sharing what appears to be his fatalism. Confronted by tendencies which he believes to be at once bad and irresistible, he inclines at times to misanthropy. Moreover, this misanthropy seems to have its source less in his reason than in his emotions; so that certain critics have found a Belphegorian taint in his own writings.

JULIEN BENDA

In theory at all events, M. Benda is not only consistently on the side of reason but he protects the word with a Socratic dialectic. Bergson proclaims that one can escape from mechanism and at the same time become vital and dynamic only by a resort to intuition, and then proceeds to identify the intuitive with the instinctive and the subrational. But the abstract type of reason that is at the basis of the mechanistic view of life, M. Benda retorts, is not the only type. Reason may also be intuitive. Sainte-Beuve, for example, is intuitive in this sense when, in his *Lundis*, he enters into the unique gift of a writer and renders it with the utmost delicacy of shading. Intuition of this kind has nothing in common with what is, according to Bergson, the ideally intuitive act — namely, that of the chick when it pecks its way through its shell.

One may admire M. Benda's perspicacity in such discriminations and yet ask if it is enough to oppose reason in any sense to the cult of a subrational intuition and the 'Belphegorism' to which it leads. According to Bergson, there are two traditions in French philosophy: on the one hand, a tradition which puts primary emphasis on intuition and derives from Pascal; on the other, a tradition which is primarily rationalistic and derives from Descartes. One would like to know what M. Benda thinks of Bergson's claim to be in the direct line of descent from Pascal. Does he suppose that when Pascal appeals from reason to something that he calls variously 'sentiment,' 'instinct,' 'heart,' these terms have the same meaning for him that they have come to have since Rousseau and the sentimentalists? The truth is that the terms refer to a superrational quality of will identified with the divine will in the form of grace, and that it is this quality of will that has been weakened by the decline of traditional religion. Faith in a higher will, as it appears in a Pascal, acted restrictively on the 'lusts' of the natural man. According to the familiar classification, the three main lusts (the 'three rivers of fire' of which Pascal speaks) are the lust of knowledge, of sensation, and of power.

The most subtle peril, according to the austere Christian, is that which arises from the lust of knowledge. M. Benda is too thorough-going an intellectual to be apprehensive of any such peril, much less to fall, as the Christian has done at times, into obscurantism. He has probably never asked himself seriously the question that seemed to Cardinal Newman the most essential of all: 'What must be the face-to-face antagonist by which to withstand and baffle... the all-corroding, all-dissolving energy of the intellect?' As for the lust of feeling, the reader of *Belphégor* is scarcely likely to accuse M. Benda of not being sufficiently on his guard against it. He has, again, in a recent work, *La Trahison des Clercs* [1] (1928), set forth the dangers of certain modern manifestations of the lust of domination. The epigraph of this work is taken from the philosopher Renouvier, a disciple of Kant: 'The world suffers from a lack of faith in a transcendent truth.' One is prompted to inquire at once whether one can secure this faith in a transcendent truth simply by an appeal to reason; whether a true transcendence does not call for the affirmation, either in the Christian or some other form, of a higher will. At all events M. Benda develops the thesis that every civilized society requires a body of 'clerks' (and by clerks he understands not merely the clergy in the

[1] English translation published at London under the title *The Great Betrayal*; same translation published at New York under the title *The Treason of the Intellectuals*.

[196]

narrower sense of the term, but thinkers, writers
and artists) who are dedicated to the service of the
something in man that transcends his material interests and animal appetites. Other ages and civilizations have had 'clerks' who were faithful to their
high vocation, often at the cost of contumely and
persecution. But in our own day the clerks have
been guilty of a 'great betrayal.' They themselves
have become secular in temper, and in consequence
have, instead of resisting the egoistic passions of the
laity, taken to flattering them. They have sided
more and more with the centrifugal forces, the
forces that array man against man, class against
class, and finally nation against nation. They have
encouraged in particular a type of patriotism that,
besides supplying themes to the votaries of Belphegor, has stimulated the will to power in a form that,
as M. Benda describes it, is close to the 'irrational
imperialism' of M. Seillière. If the clerks had been
true and not traitorous, they would, instead of
helping to inbreed differences, have rallied to the
defense of the disciplines that tend to draw men to
a common center even across national frontiers. As
a result of the clerical apostasy, M. Benda foresees

wars of zoölogical extermination. He admits, however, another possibility: men may be induced to
vent their fury of conquest not upon other men but
upon physical nature. He enlarges upon this latter
possibility in a vein that might have appealed to
Swift: 'Henceforth, united in an immense army, an
immense factory,... contemptuous of every free and
disinterested activity, thoroughly cured of faith in
any good beyond the real world,... humanity will
attain to a really grandiose control of its material
environment, to a really joyous consciousness of its
own power and grandeur. And history will smile at
the thought that Socrates and Jesus Christ died for
that race.'

M. Benda's work may be defined in its total trend
as a sweeping indictment of the modernists by a
modern. Thus far, at least, he has refused to ally
himself with the reactionaries. The position of the
modern may turn out to be untenable in the long
run, unless it can be shown to be truly constructive;
and it is on the constructive side that M. Benda is
the least satisfying. The charge has been brought
against him that the 'clerk,' as he conceives him, is
too aloof, too much 'above the mêlée.' The con-

templative life, however, may have its own justification. Furthermore, he is willing that his clerk
should, on occasion, be militant in the secular
order. The real difficulty is that M. Benda does not
give an adequate notion of the doctrine and discipline on which the clerk is to base his militancy;
nor again of the type of effort that must be put
forth in the contemplative life, if it is to be more
than a retreat into some tower of ivory. His weakness as a philosopher would appear, as I have
already hinted, to be his failure to recognize that
the opposite of the subrational is not merely the
rational but the superrational, and that this superrational and transcendent element in man is a certain quality of will. This quality of will may prove
to be alone capable of supplying a sufficient counterpoise to the various 'lusts,' including the lust of
feeling, that result from the free unfolding of man's
natural will. M. Benda's inadequacy in dealing
with the will is closely related to his drift towards
fatalism and his occasional misanthropy. Any one
who affirmed the higher will on psychological rather
than dogmatic or theological grounds might perhaps
aspire to the praise of being a constructive modern.

JULIEN BENDA

In the meanwhile, a necessary preliminary to any valid construction, must be a sound diagnosis of existing evils. It is just here — as an acute diagnostician of the modern mind and its maladies — that M. Benda has put us under obligations to him. One finds in him a combination of keen analysis with honesty and courage that is rare at the present time, or indeed at any time.

VII

THE CRITIC AND AMERICAN LIFE

A FREQUENT remark of the French about Americans is: 'They're children'; which, interpreted, means that from the French point of view Americans are childishly uncritical. The remark is relevant only in so far as it refers to general critical intelligence. In dealing with the special problems of a commercial and industrial society, Americans have shown that they can be abundantly critical. Certain Americans, for example, have developed a critical keenness in estimating the value of stocks and bonds that is nothing short of uncanny.[1] The very persons, however, who are thus keen in some particular field are,

[1] This was written before the collapse of the great common stock bubble in the autumn of 1929. It then became evident that what the financial leaders of the 'boom' period lacked was not so much expertness in their own field as general critical intelligence — especially some working knowledge of the ways of Nemesis. There were of course honorable exceptions. The late Paul M. Warburg showed that he was one of them when he remarked, apropos of the so-called business cycle, that 'it is a subject for psychologists rather than for economists.' [What is involved] 'is the answer to the question: How long — in industry, commerce and finance — does the memory of painful experiences prevent human greed and conceit from regaining control, etc.'

when confronted with questions that call for general critical intelligence, often puerile. Yet in an age like the present, which is being subjected to a constant stream of propaganda in everything from the choice of its religion to its cigarettes, general critical intelligence would seem desirable.

As a matter of fact, most persons nowadays aspire to be not critical but creative. We have not merely creative poets and novelists, but creative readers and listeners and dancers. Lately a form of creativeness has appeared that may in time swallow up all the others — creative salesmanship. The critic himself has caught the contagion and also aspires to be creative. He is supposed to become so when he receives from the creation of another, conceived as pure temperamental overflow, so vivid an impression that, when passed through his temperament, it issues forth as a fresh creation. What is eliminated in both critic and creator is any standard that is set above temperament and that therefore might interfere with their eagerness to get themselves expressed.

This notion of criticism as self-expression is important for our present subject, for it has been adopted by the writer who is, according to the

THE CRITIC AND AMERICAN LIFE

Encyclopædia Britannica,[1] 'the greatest critical force in America' — Mr. H. L. Mencken. Creative self-expression, as practiced by himself and others, has, according to Mr. Mencken, led to a salutary stirring up of the stagnant pool of American letters: 'Today for the first time in years there is strife in American criticism.... Heretics lay on boldly and the professors are forced to make some defence. Often going further they attempt counter-attacks. Ears are bitten off, noses are bloodied. There are wallops both above and below the belt.'

But it may be that criticism is something more than Mr. Mencken would have us believe, more in short than a squabble between Bohemians, each eager to capture the attention of the public for his brand of self-expression. To reduce criticism indeed to the satisfaction of a temperamental urge, to the uttering of one's gustos and disgustos (in Mr. Mencken's case chiefly the latter) is to run counter to the very etymology of the word which implies discrimination and judgment. The best one would anticipate from a writer like Mr. Mencken, possess-

[1] Thirteenth edition. In the fourteenth edition we are informed that Mr. Mencken is a satirist rather than a critic.

THE CRITIC AND AMERICAN LIFE

ing an unusual verbal virtuosity and at the same
time temperamentally irresponsible, is superior intellectual vaudeville. One must grant him, however, certain genuine critical virtues — for example,
a power of shrewd observation within rather narrow
limits. Yet the total effect of his writing is nearer to
intellectual vaudeville than to serious criticism.

The serious critic is more concerned with achieving a correct scale of values and so seeing things
proportionately than with self-expression. His essential virtue is poise. The specific benefit he
confers is to act as a moderating influence on the
opposite insanities between which mankind in the
lump is constantly tending to oscillate — oscilla-
tions that Luther compares to the reelings of a
drunken peasant on horseback. The critic's survey
of any particular situation may very well seem
satirical. The complaint that Mr. Mencken is too
uniformly disgruntled in his survey of the American
situation rather misses the point. Behind the pleas
for more constructiveness it is usually easy to detect
the voice of the booster. A critic who did not get
beyond a correct diagnosis of existing evils might
be very helpful. If Mr. Mencken has fallen short

of being such a diagnostician, the failure is due not to his excess of severity but to his lack of discrimination.

The standards with reference to which men have discriminated in the past have been largely traditional. The outstanding fact of the present period, on the other hand, has been the weakening of traditional standards. An emergency has arisen not unlike that with which Socrates sought to cope in ancient Athens. Anyone who is untraditional and seeks at the same time to be discriminating must almost necessarily own Socrates as his master. As is well known, Socrates sought above all to be discriminating in his use of general terms. Before allowing one's imagination and finally one's conduct to be controlled by a general term, it would seem wise to submit it to a Socratic scrutiny.

It is, therefore, unfortunate that at a time like the present, which plainly calls for a Socrates, we should instead have got a Mencken. One may take as an example of Mr. Mencken's failure to discriminate adequately, his attitude towards the term that for several generations past has been governing the imagination of multitudes — democracy. His view of democracy is simply that of Rousseau turned upside down, and nothing, as has been remarked, resembles a hollow so much as a swelling. A distinction of which he has failed to recognize the importance is that between a direct or unlimited and a constitutional democracy. In the latter we probably have the best thing in the world. The former, on the other hand, as all thinkers of any penetration from Plato and Aristotle down have perceived, leads to the loss of liberty and finally to the rise of some form of despotism. The two conceptions of democracy involve not merely incompatible views of government but ultimately of human nature. The desire of the constitutional democrat for institutions that act as checks on the immediate will of the people implies a similar dualism in the individual — a higher self that acts restrictively on his ordinary and impulsive self. The partisan of unlimited democracy on the other hand is an idealist in the sense the term assumed in connection with the so-called romantic movement. His faith in the people is closely related to the doctrine of natural goodness proclaimed by the sentimentalists of the eighteenth century and itself marking an extreme recoil from the dogma of total depravity. The doctrine of natural goodness favors the free temperamental expansion that I have already noticed in speaking of the creative critic.

It is of the utmost importance, however, if one is to understand Mr. Mencken, to discriminate between two types of temperamentalist — the soft and sentimental type, who cherishes various 'ideals,' and the hard, or Nietzschean type, who piques himself on being realistic. As a matter of fact, if one sees in the escape from traditional controls merely an opportunity to live temperamentally, it would seem advantageous to pass promptly from the idealistic to the Nietzschean phase, sparing oneself as many as possible of the intermediary disillusions. It is at all events undeniable that the rise of Menckenism has been marked by a certain collapse of romantic idealism in the political field and elsewhere. The numerous disillusions that have supervened upon the War have provided a favoring atmosphere.

The symptoms of Menckenism are familiar: a certain hardness and smartness and disposition to rail at everything that, rightly or wrongly, is established and respected; a tendency to identify the real with what Mr. Mencken terms 'the cold and clammy facts' and to assume that the only alternative to facing these facts is to fade away into sheer romantic unreality. These and similar traits are becoming so widely diffused that, whatever one's opinion of Mr. Mencken as a writer and thinker, one must grant him representativeness. He is a chief prophet at present of those who deem themselves emancipated but who are, according to Mr. Brownell, merely unbuttoned.

The crucial point in any case is one's attitude towards the principle of control. Those who stand for this principle in any form or degree are dismissed by the emancipated as reactionaries or, still graver reproach, as Puritans. Mr. Mencken would have us believe that the historical Puritan was not even sincere in his moral rigorism, but was given to 'lamentable transactions with loose women and fiery jugs.' This may serve as a sample of the assertions, picturesquely indiscriminate, by which a writer wins immediate notoriety at the expense of his permanent reputation. The facts about the Puritan happen to be complex and need to be dealt with very Socratically. It has been affirmed that the point of view of the Puritan was stoical rather than truly Christian, and the affirmation is not wholly false. The present discussion of the relationship between Puritanism and the rise of capitalism with its glorification of the acquisitive life also has its justification. It is likewise a fact that the Puritan was from the outset unduly concerned with reforming others as well as himself, and this trait relates him to the humanitarian meddler or 'wowser' of the present day, who is Mr. Mencken's pet aversion.

Yet it remains true that awe and reverence and humility are Christian virtues and that there was some survival of these virtues in the Puritan. For a representative Puritan like Jonathan Edwards they were inseparable from the illumination of grace, from what he terms 'a divine and super-natural light.' In the passage from the love and fear of God of an Edwards to the love and service of man professed by the humanitarian, something has plainly dropped out, something that is very near the center. What has tended to disappear is the inner life with the special type of control it imposes. With the decline of this inner control there has been an increasing resort to outer control. Instead of the genuine Puritan we then have the humanitarian legalist who passes innumerable laws for the control of people who refuse to control themselves. The activity of our uplifters is scarcely suggestive of any 'divine and supernatural light.' Here is a discrimination of the first importance that has been obscured by the muddy thinking of our half-baked intelligentsia. One is thus kept from perceiving the real problem, which is to retain the inner life, even though one refuse to accept the theological nightmare with which the Puritan associated it. More is involved in the failure to solve this problem than the Puritan tradition. It is the failure of our contemporary life in general. Yet, unless some solution is reached by a full and free exercise of the critical spirit, one remains a mere modernist and not a thoroughgoing and complete modern; for the modern spirit and the critical spirit are in their essence one.

What happens, when one sets out to deal with questions of this order without sufficient depth of reflection and critical maturity, may be seen in Mr.

THE CRITIC AND AMERICAN LIFE

Sinclair Lewis's *Elmer Gantry*. He has been lured from art into the writing of a wild diatribe which, considered even as such, is largely beside the mark. If the Protestant Church is at present threatened with bankruptcy, it is not because it has produced an occasional Elmer Gantry. The true reproach it has incurred is that, in its drift toward modernism, it has lost its grip not merely on certain dogmas but, simultaneously, on the facts of human nature. It has failed above all to carry over in some modern and critical form the truth of a dogma that unfortunately receives much support from these facts — the dogma of original sin. At first sight Mr. Mencken would appear to have a conviction of evil — when, for example, he reduces democracy in its essential aspect to a 'combat between jackals and jackasses' — that establishes at least one bond between him and the austere Christian.

The appearance, however, is deceptive. The Christian is conscious above all of the 'old Adam' in himself: hence his humility. The effect of Mr. Mencken's writing, on the other hand, is to produce pride rather than humility, a pride ultimately based on flattery. The reader, especially the young and callow reader, identifies himself imaginatively with Mr. Mencken and conceives of himself as a sort of morose and sardonic divinity surveying from some superior altitude an immeasurable expanse of 'boobs.' This attitude will not seem especially novel to anyone who has traced the modern movement. One is reminded in particular of Flaubert, who showed a diligence in collecting bourgeois imbecilities comparable to that displayed by Mr. Mencken in his *Americana*. Flaubert's discovery that one does not add to one's happiness in this way would no doubt be dismissed by Mr. Mencken as irrelevant, for he has told us that he does not believe in happiness. Another discovery of Flaubert's may seem to him more worthy of consideration. 'By dint of railing at idiots,' Flaubert reports, 'one runs the risk of becoming idiotic oneself.'

It may be that the only way to escape from the unduly complacent cynicism of Mr. Mencken and his school is to reaffirm once more the truths of the inner life. In that case it would seem desirable to disengage, so far as possible, the principle of control on which the inner life finally depends from mere creeds and traditions and assert it as a psychological fact; a fact, moreover, that is neither 'cold' nor 'clammy.' The coldness and clamminess of much so called realism arises from its failure to give this fact due recognition. A chief task, indeed, of the Socratic critic would be to rescue the noble term 'realist' from its present degradation. A view of reality that overlooks the element in man that moves in an opposite direction from mere temperament, the specifically human factor in short, may prove to be singularly one-sided. Is the Puritan, John Milton, when he declares that 'he who reigns within himself and rules passions, desires, and fears is more than a king,' less real than Mr. Theodore Dreiser when he discourses in his peculiar dialect of 'those rearranging chemisms upon which all the morality or immorality of the world is based?'

As a matter of fact, according to the degree and nature of the exercise of the principle of control, one may distinguish two main types of realism which may be denominated respectively religious and humanistic: as the principle of control falls into abeyance, a third type tends to emerge, which may be termed naturalistic realism. That the decline of the traditional controls has been followed by a lapse to the naturalistic level is indubitable. The characteristic evils of the present age arise from unrestraint and violation of the law of measure and not, as our modernists would have us believe, from the tyranny of taboos and traditional inhibitions. The facts cry to heaven. The delicate adjustment that is required between the craving for emancipation and the need of control has been pointed out once for all by Goethe, speaking not as a Puritan but as a clear-eyed man of the world. Everything, he says, that liberates the spirit without a corresponding growth in self-mastery is pernicious. This one sentence would seem to cover the case of our 'flaming youth' rather completely.

The movement in the midst of which we are still living was from its inception unsound in its dealing with the principle of control. It is vain to expect from the dregs of this movement what its 'first sprightly running failed to give.' Mr. Carl Sandburg speaks of the 'marvelous rebellion of man at all signs reading "Keep off."' An objection to this purely insurrectional attitude is that, as a result of its endless iteration during the past century and more, it has come to savor too strongly of what has

been called 'the humdrum of revolt.' A more
serious objection to the attitude is that it encourages
an unrestricted and merely temperamental liberty
which, paradoxically enough at first sight, affords
the modern man no avenue of escape from the web
that is being woven about him by the scientific
determinist.

Realists of the current type are in point of fact
intimately allied with the psychologists — glan-
dular, behavioristic, and psycho-analytical — who,
whatever their divergences among themselves,
unite in their deterministic trend and therefore
clash fundamentally with both religious and humanistic realists. The proper method of proce-
dure in defending the freedom of the will would
seem to be to insist upon it as a fact of experience,
a fact so primary that the position of the determinist involves an evasion of one of the immediate
data of consciousness in favor of a metaphysical
dream. What is genuinely experimental in naturalistic psychology should of course be received with
respect; but the facts of which it takes account in
its experiments are unimportant compared with the
facts it either neglects or denies. Practically it is

running into grotesque extremes of pseudo-science that make of it a shining mark for the Socratic critic.

Here at all events is the issue on which all other issues finally hinge; for until the question of moral freedom — the question whether man is a responsible agent or only the plaything of his impulses and impressions — is decided, nothing is decided; and to decide the question under existing circumstances calls for the keenest critical discrimination. Creation that is not sufficiently supported by such discrimination is likely to prove premature.

One may illustrate from Mr. Dreiser's *American Tragedy*, hailed in certain quarters as the 'Mount Everest' of recent fiction. He has succeeded in producing in this work something genuinely harrowing; but one is harrowed to no purpose. One has in more than full measure the tragic qualm but without the final relief and enlargement of spirit that true tragedy succeeds somehow in giving, and that without resort to explicit moralizing. It is hardly worth while to struggle through eight hundred and more very pedestrian pages to be left at the end with a feeling of sheer oppression. The explanation of this

oppression is that Mr. Dreiser does not rise sufficiently above the level of 'rearranging chemisms,'
in other words, of animal behavior. Tragedy may
admit fate — Greek tragedy admits it — but not of
the naturalistic variety. Confusion on this point
may compromise in the long run the reputation of
writers more eminent than Mr. Dreiser — for example, of Thomas Hardy. Fatalism of the naturalistic type is responsible in large measure for the
atmosphere of futility and frustration that hangs
heavily over so much contemporary writing. One
finally comes to feel with a recent poet that 'dust'
is the common source from which

stream
The cricket's cry and Dante's dream.

Anyone who admits reality only in what derives
from the dust, whether in a cricket or a Dante,
must, from the point of view of the religious or the
humanistic realist, be prepared to make substantial
sacrifices. In the first place, he must sacrifice the
depth and subtlety that arise from the recognition
in some form of the duality of man's nature. For
the interest that may arise from the portrayal of the
conflict between a law of the spirit and a law of the

members, the inordinate interest in sex for its own sake promoted by most of the so-called realists is a rather shabby substitute. A merely naturalistic realism also involves the sacrifice of beauty in almost any sense of that elusive term. Closely related to this sacrifice is the sacrifice of delicacy, elevation, and distinction. The very word realism has come to connote the opposite of these qualities. When we learn, for example, that someone has written a realistic study of a great man, we are sure in advance that he has devoted his main effort to proving that 'Plutarch lied.' The more the great man is reduced to the level of commonplace or worse, the more we feel he has been 'humanized.'

Mr. Sherwood Anderson has argued ingeniously that, inasmuch as we ourselves are crude, our literature, if it is not to be unreal and factitious, should be crude likewise. But the writer who hopes to achieve work of importance cannot afford to be too deeply immersed in the atmosphere of the special place and passing moment. Still less can he afford to make us feel, as writers like Mr. Anderson and Mr. Dreiser and Mr. Sinclair Lewis do, that, if there were any lack of vulgarity in what they are depicting, they would be capable of supplying the defect from their own abundance. More is involved here than mere loss of distinction. We have come, indeed, to the supreme sacrifice that every writer must make who does not transcend a naturalistic realism. He must forego the hope of the enduring appeal — the hope that every writer worthy of his salt cherishes in some degree. In the absence of humanistic or religious standards, he is prone to confound the real with the welter of the actual, and so to miss the 'grandeur of generality.'

Certain books in the current mode are so taken up with the evanescent surfaces of life that they will survive, if at all, not as literature but as sociological documents. The very language in which they are written will, in a generation or two, require a glossary. So far from imposing an orderly pattern on the raw material of experience, they rather emphasize the lack of pattern. The resulting effect, to borrow a phrase from the late Stephen Crane, who has had a marked influence on the recent movement, is that of a 'cluttered incoherency.' As an extreme example of the tendency one may cite *Manhattan Transfer* by John Dos Passos. In the name of reality, Mr. Dos Passos has perpetrated a literary nightmare. Such a work would seem to have slight value even as a sociological document; unless, indeed, one is prepared to admit that contemporary Manhattan is inhabited chiefly by epileptic Bohemians.

'It is as much a trade,' says La Bruyère, 'to make a book as it is to make a clock'; in short, literature is largely a matter of technique. The technique of *Manhattan Transfer* is as dubious as its underlying philosophy. Neither can be justified save on the assumption that the aim of art is to exaggerate the clutter and incoherency of the mundane spectacle instead of eliciting its deeper meaning. Technique counts for even more in poetry than in prose. It would be possible to base on technical grounds alone a valid protest against the present preposterous overestimate of Walt Whitman. Fundamental questions need, in these very untraditional days, to be critically elucidated with a view to right definition if the poet is not to lack technique or still worse, if he is not, like certain recent practitioners of free verse, to be hagridden by a false technique. It evidently concerns both the form and substance of poetry, whether one define it with Aristotle as the portrayal of representative human action, or whether one define it with Mr. Carl Sandburg as a 'mystic, sensuous mathematics of fire, smokestacks, waffles, pansies, people, and purple sunsets.'

There is no doubt much in the America of to-day that suggests a jazzy impressionism. Still our naturalistic deliquescence has probably not gone so far as one might infer from poetry like that of Mr. Sandburg or fiction like that of Mr. Dos Passos. The public response to some of the realistic novels has been considerable: allowance must be made however for the *succès de scandale*, also for the skill attained by the modern publisher in the art of merchandizing. The reputation of certain books one might mention may be regarded as a triumph of 'creative' advertising. What has been created is a mirage of masterpieces where no masterpieces are. It is well also to remember in regard to some of the works that have been most discussed that, so far from being an authentic reflection of the American scene, they are rather a belated echo of certain European movements. For it is as certain that in our literary and artistic modes we follow Europe

[221]

usually at an interval of from five to forty years — as it is that we lead Europe in our bathtubs and sanitary plumbing. Anyone who resided in Paris in the nineties and later in America, will, as I can testify from personal experience, have the sense of having lived through the same literary fads twice. Mr. Dreiser reminds one of Zola and his school. The technique of Mr. Dos Passos recalls that of the Goncourts. Our experimenters in free verse have followed in the wake not merely of Walt Whitman but of the French symbolists, and so on.

We shall presently begin to hear of certain new developments in French literature and critical thought that point, though indecisively as yet, to a radical departure from what has been the main current since the eighteenth century and in some respects since the Renaissance. It is well that we should become familiar with the writers who reveal in different ways this latest trend — notably with Maritain, Maurras, Lasserre, Seillière, and Benda; for they give evidence of a quality of cerebration that is rare in our own literati. At the same time we should not adopt with our usual docility the total outlook of any of these writers: for no one of them has worked out a point of view exactly adapted to our requirements. In general, it is not fitting that a great nation at the very height of its power should go on indefinitely trailing after Europe. It is time for us to initiate something of our own. This does not mean that we should proceed forthwith to inbreed our own 'originality.' It means almost the exact opposite. The most original thing one could do nowadays would be to question the whole theory of originality as mere temperamental overflow and self-expression that has prevailed from the 'geniuses' of the eighteenth century down to one of our youthful and very minor bards who aspires to 'spill his bright illimitable soul.'

A genuinely critical survey would make manifest that the unsatisfactoriness of our creative effort is due to a lack of the standards that culture alone can supply. Our cultural crudity and insignificance can be traced in turn to the inadequacy of our education, especially our higher education. Mr. Mencken's attack on the 'professors' is therefore largely justified; for if the professors were performing their function properly Mr. Mencken himself would not be possible. One must add in common justice that the professors themselves, or at least some of them, are becoming aware that all is not well with existing conditions. One could not ask anything more perspicacious than the following paragraph from a recent report of Committee G to the American Association of University Professors:

American education has suffered from the domination, conscious or unconscious, direct or indirect, of political and sentimental, as well as educational, theories that are demonstrably false. If the views of some men are to prevail the intellectual life of the country is doomed; everybody except the sheer idiot is to go to college and pursue chiefly sociology, nature study, child study, and community service — and we shall have a society unique only in its mediocrity, ignorance and vulgarity. It will not do to dismiss lightly even so extreme a view as this; it is too indicative. Such influences are very strong, their pressure is constant; and if education has largely failed in America it has been due primarily to them.

In short, as a result of the encroachments of an equalitarian democracy, the standards of our higher education have suffered in two distinct particulars: first, as regards the quality of students; second, as regards the quality of the studies these students pursue. The first of these evils is generally recognized. There is even some prospect of remedial measures. Certain institutions, Harvard, for example, without being as yet severely selective, are becoming more critical of the incompetent student. On the other hand, there seems to be less hope than ever of any righting of the second and more serious evil — the failure to distinguish qualitatively between studies. The main drift is still towards what one may term the blanket degree. (Dartmouth, for example, has just merged its bachelor of arts and bachelor of science.) Yet rather than blur certain distinctions it would have been better, one might suppose, to use up all the letters of the alphabet devising new degrees to meet the real or supposed educational needs of the modern man. To bestow the A.B. degree indiscriminately on a student for whom education has meant primarily a specialization in chemistry and on one for whom it has meant primarily an assimilation of the masterpieces of Greek literature is to empty it of any effective meaning. At the present rate, indeed, the time may come when the A.B. will not throw much more light on the cultural quality of its recipient than it would, if, as has been suggested, it were bestowed on every American child at birth.

It goes without saying that those who have been lowering and confusing educational standards have been profuse in their professions of 'service.' A critical examination, not merely of American education but of American life at the present time will almost necessarily hinge on this term. The attitude of the Socratic critic towards it is not to be confounded with that of Mr. Mencken and the 'hardboiled' contingent. 'When a gang of real estate agents,' says Mr. Mencken, 'bond salesmen, and automobile dealers gets together to sob for Service, it takes no Freudian to surmise that someone is about to be swindled.' But if one entertain doubts about this current American gospel, why waste one's ammunition on any such small fry? Other and more exalted personages than the members of the Rotary Club at Zenith have, in Mr. Sinclair Lewis's elegant phrase, been 'yipping for Service.' If one is to deal with this idea of service Socratically, one needs to consider it in its relation to the two figures who have rightly been taken to be the most representative in our cultural background — Benjamin Frank-

lin and Jonathan Edwards. Franklin's idea of service is already humanitarian. Edwards' idea is still
traditionally Christian — service not of man but of
God. What Franklin stood for is flourishing prodi-
giously at the present moment, so much so that he
may perhaps be defined in his chief line of influence
as the great superrotarian. What Edwards stood
for is, on the other hand, largely obsolete or survives
only in the form of habits, which, lacking doctrinal
support, are steadily declining along with the whole
Puritan culture.

Intermediary types are possible. One may in
one's character reflect the Puritan background and
at the same time in one's idea of service derive
rather from Franklin. Precisely that combination
is found in the most influential of our recent educational leaders — the late President Eliot. A
legitimate admiration for his personal qualities
should not interfere with the keenest critical
scrutiny of his views about education, for the two
things stand in no necessary connection. Practically this means to scrutinize the humanitarian
idealism that he probably did more than any other
man of his generation to promote. In this respect

most of the heads of our institutions of learning have been and still are understudies of President Eliot.

In an address on the occasion of his ninetieth birthday President Eliot warned his hearers against introspection, lest it divert them from a wholehearted devotion to service. Between this attitude and a religious or humanistic attitude there is a clash of first principles. Both humanism and religion require introspection as a prerequisite of the inner life and its appropriate activity. With the disappearance of this activity what is left is the outer activity of the utilitarian, and this leads straight to the one-sided cult of material efficiency and finally to the standardization that is, according to nearly all foreign critics and many of our own, a chief American danger. We cannot return to the introspection of the Puritan. We shudder at the theology an Edwards would impose as the condition of his 'divine and supernatural light.' Yet it does not follow, as I have already suggested, that we should reject the inner life itself along with this theology. One may recognize innumerable incidental advantages in the gospel of service and yet harbor an uneasy suspicion withal that in the passage from the older religion to the modern humanitarian dispensation something vital has disappeared, something for which neither the outer working of the utilitarian nor again the expansive sympathy of the sentimentalist can offer an equivalent.

The problem of the inner life is very much bound up with two other problems that are now pressing for solution in our higher education and have as yet found none: the problem of the specialist and the problem of leisure. The man of leisure is engaged in an inner and specifically human form of activity, a form that is, according to Aristotle, needful if he is to compass the end of ends — his own happiness. The question is whether one should consent like the specialist to forego this activity and to live partially and as a mere instrument for the attainment of some outer end — even though this end be the progress of humanity. We are beginning to hear a great deal nowadays about the 'menace' of leisure. It has been estimated that with the perfecting of mechanical devices the man of the future will be able to satisfy his material wants by working not more than four hours a day. It is vain to anticipate that the rank and file will use this release from outer activity intelligently unless the leaders, notably those in high academic station, show the way. The notion of true leisure is the ultimate source of the standards of any education that deserves to be called liberal. When even a few of our college and university presidents show that they are thinking to some purpose on the nature of leisure it will be time enough to talk of 'America's coming of age.'

As it is, our institutions of learning seem to be becoming more and more hotbeds of 'idealism.' Their failure, on the whole, to achieve standards as something quite distinct from ideals, on the one hand, and standardization, on the other, may prove a fact of sinister import for the future of American civilization. The warfare that is being waged at the present time by Mr. Sinclair Lewis and others against a standardized Philistinism continues in the main the protest that has been made for several generations past by the temperamentalists, hard or soft, against the mechanizing of life by the utilitarian. This protest has been, and is likely to continue to be, ineffectual. The fruitful opposite of the standardized Philistine is not the Bohemian, nor again the hard temperamentalist or superman, as Mr. Mencken conceives him, but the man of leisure. Leisure involves an inner effort with reference to standards that is opposed to the sheer expansion of temperament, as it is to every other form of sheer expansion.

Perhaps a reason why the standards of the humanist are less popular in this country than the ideals of the humanitarian is that these standards set bounds to the acquisitive life; whereas it seems possible to combine a perfect idealism with an orgy of unrestricted commercialism. It is well for us to try to realize how we appear to others in this matter. Our growing unpopularity abroad is due no doubt in part to envy of our material success, but it also arises from the proneness of the rest of the world to judge us, not by the way we feel about ourselves, but by our actual performance. If we are in our own eyes a nation of idealists, we are, according to a recent French critic, M. André Siegfried,[1] a 'nation of Pharisees.' The European,

[1] See his volume *Les États-Unis d'aujourd'hui* (1927), translated under the title *America Comes of Age*.

M. Siegfried would have us believe, still has a concern for the higher values of civilization, whereas the American is prepared to sacrifice these values ruthlessly to mass production and material efficiency. It is easy to detect under this assumption the latest form of a 'certain condescension in foreigners.' The breakdown of cultural standards is European as well as American. It is not clear that M. Siegfried himself has an adequate notion of the form of effort that can alone serve as a counterpoise to the one-sided activity of the utilitarian. At the same time his anatomy of our favorite ideal of service is not without interest. This ideal opposes no effective barrier to our expansiveness. An unchecked expansiveness on the national scale is always imperialistic. Among the ingredients of a possible American imperialism M. Siegfried enumerates the American's 'great self-satisfaction, his rather brutal sense of his own interests, and *the consciousness, still more dangerous, of his "duties" towards humanity.'* M. Siegfried admits however that our imperialism is likely to be of a new and subtle essence, not concerned primarily with territorial aggrandizement.

THE CRITIC AND AMERICAN LIFE

A proper discussion of Mr. Siegfried's position as well as of other issues I have been raising would transcend the limits of an essay. My end has been accomplished if I have justified in some measure the statement with which I started as to the importance of cultivating a general critical intelligence. James Russell Lowell's dictum that before having an American literature we must have an American criticism was never truer than it is today. The obvious reply to those who call for more creation and less criticism is that one needs to be critical above all in examining what now passes for creation. A scrutiny of this kind would, I have tried to show, extend beyond the bounds of literature to various aspects of our national life and would converge finally on our higher education.

We cannot afford to accept as a substitute for this true criticism the self-expression of Mr. Mencken and his school, unless indeed we are to merit the comment that is, I am told, made on us by South Americans: 'They are not a very serious people!' To be sure, the reader may reflect that I am myself a critic, or would-be critic. I can only express the hope that, in my magnifying of the critical function, I do not offer too close a parallel to the dancing-master in Molière who averred, it will be remembered, that 'all the mistakes of men, the fatal reverses that fill the world's annals, the shortcomings of statesmen, and the blunders of great captains arise from not knowing how to dance.'

VIII

ROMANTICISM AND THE ORIENT

THE special danger of the present time is an increasing material contact between national and racial groups that remain spiritually alien. The chief obstacle to a better understanding between East and West in particular is a certain type of occidental who is wont to assume almost unconsciously that the East has everything to learn from the West and little or nothing to give in return. One may distinguish three main forms of this assumption of superiority on the part of the occidental: first, the assumption of racial superiority, an almost mystical faith in the preëminent virtues of the white peoples (especially Nordic blonds) as compared with the brown or yellow races; second, the assumption of superiority based on the achievements of physical science and the type of 'progress' it has promoted, a tendency to regard as a general inferiority the inferiority of the oriental in material efficiency; third, the assumption of religious superiority, the tendency, less marked now than formerly, to dismiss non-Christian Asiatics *en masse* as 'heathen,' or else to recognize value in their religious beliefs only in so far as they conform to the pattern set by Christianity. Asiatics for their part are ready enough to turn to account the discoveries of Western science, but they are even less disposed than they were before the Great War to admit the moral superiority of the West. A certain revulsion of feeling seems to be taking place even in Japan which has gone farther than any other oriental land in its borrowings from the Occident.

On any comprehensive view, indeed, Asiatics, so far from having a mean estimate of themselves, have had their own conceit of superiority, not only with reference to occidentals, but with reference to one another. Many Hindus have held in the past, some no doubt still hold, that true spirituality has never appeared in the world save on the sacred soil of India. No country, again, not even ancient Greece, has been more firmly convinced than China that it alone was civilized. A statesman of the Tang period addressed to the throne a memorial against Buddhism which begins as follows: 'This Buddha was a barbarian.' One of the traditional names of China, 'All-under-Heaven' (Poo-Tien-shia), is itself sufficiently eloquent.

In general, Asia offers cultural groups so widely divergent that one may ask if there is not something artificial in any attempt to contrast an Asiatic with a European or Western point of view. An attempt of this kind was made at Paris a few years ago in the form of a symposium (*Les Appels de l'Orient*) to which about one hundred and forty French and foreign writers and scholars contributed. According to one of these contributors, M. Sylvain Lévi, professor of Sanscrit at the Collège de France, it is absurd to bring together under one label 'a Syrian of Beyrut, an Iranian of Persia, a Brahmin of Benares, a pariah of the Deccan, a merchant of Canton, a mandarin of Peking, a lama of Thibet, a yakut of Siberia, a daimio of Japan, a cannibal of Sumatra, etc.' One may indeed affirm almost anything of Asia in general compared with the Occident in general. One may even, like Dr. Frederic Ives Carpenter in his recent volume, *Emerson and Asia*, discover an oriental element in the dramas of Eugene O'Neill!

ROMANTICISM AND THE ORIENT

The question of East *versus* West may, nevertheless, turn out to have a very weighty meaning if properly defined and limited. Several contributors to the Paris symposium show some inkling of what this meaning is. They are helped to their sense of the contrast between Europe and Asia by another continental contrast — that between Europe and America; and here they are in substantial agreement. America stands for the purely industrial and utilitarian view of life, the cult of power and machinery and material comfort. It is in order to escape from this baleful excess of Americanism that Europe is inclined to turn towards the East. 'Europe,' we read in the symposium, 'is, as a result of her almost mortal sufferings of recent years, ready to bow her head and humble herself. It will then be possible for oriental influences to make themselves felt. An immense continent will remain the refuge and the fortress of the occidental spirit: the whole of America will harden herself and proudly close her mind, whereas Europe will heed the lesson of the Orient.' One may perhaps sum up the sense of passages of this kind by saying that in its pursuit of the truths of the natural order Europe has come to neglect the truths of humility — the truths of the inner life. In the literal sense of the word, it has lost its orientation, for it originally received those truths from the Orient (*Lux ex Oriente*). One remembers Matthew Arnold's account of this former contact between East and West; first, the impact of a Europe drunk with power upon Asia:

> The East bowed low before the blast
> In patient, deep disdain;
> She let the legions thunder past,
> And plunged in thought again.

And finally the heeding of the voice of the East, in other words the acceptance of the truths of the inner life in their Christian form, by a Europe that had grown weary of her own materialism:

> She heard it, the victorious West,
> In sword and crown arrayed,
> She felt the void that mined her breast,
> She shivered and obeyed.

The problems that arise today in connection with the relations of East and West are far more complex than they were in Graeco-Roman times. The East now means not merely the Near East, but even more the Far East. Moreover, the East, both Near and Far, is showing itself less inclined than formerly to bow before the imperialistic aggression of the Occident 'in patient, deep disdain.' On the contrary, a type of nationalistic self-assertion is beginning to appear in various oriental lands that is only too familiar to us in the West. Japan in particular has been disposing of her Buddhas as curios and going in for battleships. The lust of domination, which is almost the ultimate fact of human nature, has been so armed in the Occident with the machinery of scientific efficiency that the Orient seems to have no alternative save to become efficient in the same way or be reduced to economic and political vassalage. This alternative has been pressing with special acuteness on China, the pivotal country of the Far East. Under the impact of the West, an ethos that has endured for thousands of years has been crumbling amid a growing spiritual bewilderment. In short, the Orient itself is losing its orientation.

The essence of this orientation, as I have already suggested, may be taken to be the affirmation in the religious form of the truths of the inner life. Our interpretation of this religious side of the East has often been unduly colored during the past century or more by romanticism. I am especially struck by this romantic misinterpretation in the case of the Orient of which I have made some first-hand study, namely, ancient India, more particularly Buddhist India. The matter is of some consequence, if it be true, as I am inclined to think, that Buddha is the ultimate Oriental.

I

I take up first the more superficial aspects of romantic orientalism. What interests the romantic in the East as elsewhere is the picturesque surfaces of life rather than its constant elements. This pursuit of local color is what one finds in the volumes of the early romantics dealing with the East — for example, in *Les Orientales* of Victor Hugo. It is the Orient, says Professor W. F. Giese of this latter work, seen from Les Batignolles: 'turbaned Turks, piratical Greeks, lovely odalisks, glittering scimitars, comparadjis, spahis, timariots, bloody janissaries, black eunuchs, scented harems, azure seas with women in sacks splashing into them from the windows of marble palaces, wars, murders, massacres — and pictures.' Nowadays anyone with a thirst for the exotic can satisfy it in a more authentic form by taking a world cruise or at the very least by turning the pages of the magazine *Asia*.

A more important romantic trait for our subject is the desire to escape from an unpalatable present into some land of heart's desire. The romantic not infrequently places the bower of dreams into which he flees from the here and now in the Orient. Here is an extreme example from the Paris symposium. 'As for me,' says Mme. Alice Louis-Barthou, 'it is very simple. I look upon the Occident with abomination. It represents for me fog, grayness, chill, machinery, murderous science, factories with all the vices, the triumph of noise, of hustling, of ugliness.... The Orient is calm, peace, beauty, color, mystery, charm, sunlight, joy, ease of life and revery; in fine the exact opposite of our hateful and grotesque civilization. I am reactionary, retrograde, and antediluvian as much as one can be. So you must not ask my opinion on these matters. If I had my way, I should have a Chinese Wall built between the Orient and the Occident to keep the latter from poisoning the former; I should have the heads of all the giaours cut off, and I should go and live where you can see clearly and where there are no Europeans. *Voilà!*'

The romantic quality of imagination that appears in such passages has been combined since Rousseau with the cult of a subrational spontaneity. This Rousseauistic romanticism is precisely the type one finds in the Schlegels who actually founded the romantic school in Germany (1798–1800) and were at the same time pioneers in interpreting India to the West. The ultimate richness of the romantic imagination, said Friedrich Schlegel, will be found in India. The influence of his *Language and Wisdom of the Hindus* (1808) was far-reaching. The primitivistic coloring that the whole subject took about this time can be traced in the philosophy of Schopenhauer who looked upon himself as a disciple of the Hindus. One of the most remarkable achievements of Schopenhauer and other primitivists is to have converted Buddha, in reality one of the most alert and vigorous figures of whom we have historical record, and withal one of the most cheerful, into a heavy-eyed, pessimistic dreamer. The Rousseauism that appears in the novels of Tolstoy and other

[243]

Russians has been frequently put under the patronage of this subrational Buddha. 'Under different names and figures,' says the Vicomte de Vogüé, 'every Russian writer is going to hold up for our admiration this vegetative form of existence. The last word of human wisdom is the sanctification, the apotheosis of the elementary brute, conceived as good and vaguely fraternal.' The final source of this cult of the simple life, M. de Vogüé goes on to say, is the 'gospel of Buddha.'[1]

This primitivistic type of romanticism appears also in the poems of Leconte de Lisle from whom many Frenchmen get their notions of India. Leconte de Lisle combines a superlative sense for the picturesque surfaces of life with an extreme nostalgia, and all without the perception of any unity behind the illusory veil of the senses ($M\bar{a}y\bar{a}$), a perception that in genuine Hindu philosophy is almost an obsession. Americans are supposed to be incapable of grasping the true spirit of the East. Yet I venture to affirm without fear of being contradicted by those who have a first-hand knowledge of the documents that Emerson has put more of India into

[1] Vogüé, *Le Roman russe*, p. 312.

his *Brahma* than Leconte de Lisle into poems like *Bhagavat* and *Çunacêpa.*

II

Probably most of us get our ideas of India not from German or French sources but from a living English romanticist, Rudyard Kipling. Kipling shows the usual romantic interest in the primitive and the subrational; only he is less inclined than the earlier primitivists to see in the instinctive the source of pity and more inclined to see in it the source of strength whether in the individual or the race. In this aspect he may indeed be defined as a romantic imperialist. If I were attempting a complete estimate of Kipling, I should have to add that he combines this imperialism in a way in which only an Englishman can combine incompatibles with an Hebraic sense of righteousness. Kipling has an eye for vivid and picturesque contrasts, especially the racial contrasts that arise in the Anglo-Indian East, with a corresponding weakness in rendering what is normal and representative in human nature. His poetry also supplies examples of nostalgia. When in England, Kipling (at least the poetical Kipling) longs to be in India; when in India, he longs to be in England. One is reminded at times of the old song:

> Oh, that I were where I would be,
> Then would I be where I am not;
> Here am I where I must be,
> Where I would be I cannot.

One may cite *In Springtime* as an example of a poem in which he blends happily the two main romantic motifs of nostalgia and local color:

My garden blazes brightly with the rosebush and the peach,
And the *köil* sings above it, in the *siris* by the well.
From the creeper-covered trellis comes the squirrel's chattering speech,
And the blue-jay screams and flutters where the cheery *satbhai* dwell,
But the rose has lost its fragrance, and the *köil's* note is strange;
I am sick of endless sunshine, sick of blossom-burdened bough.
Give me back the leafless woodlands where the winds of springtime range —
Give me back one day in England, for it's spring in England now!

An even more familiar example of nostalgia in Kipling, an example almost too familiar to quote, is

ROMANTICISM AND THE ORIENT

Mandalay, a poem in which he has celebrated the longing of the British private for a 'neater, sweeter maiden, in a cleaner, greener land.' The essential passage, it will be remembered, is the following:

Ship me somewheres east of Suez where the best is like the
    worst,
Where there aren't no Ten Commandments, an' a man can
    raise a thirst;
For the temple bells are callin', an' it's there that I would
    be —
By the old Moulmein Pagoda, lookin' lazy at the sea —

If the temple bells are calling the British private to 'raise a thirst,' to what, one may inquire, are they calling the native Burman? Surely not to be 'lazy' and irresponsible. Kipling himself would no doubt warn us against pursuing any such unprofitable inquiry, in virtue of the principle that 'East is East and West is West, and never the twain shall meet.' The fact is that they are meeting more and more, with the attendant danger that this meeting will be only on the material level. Kipling's line is rightfully resented by orientals: it is true about in the sense that John is John and James is James, and never the twain shall meet, or, if there is any dif-

[247]

ference between the two statements, it is one of degree and not of kind.

If we refuse, then, to admit that the point of view of Buddhist Burma is necessarily unintelligible to us and turn for information to the authentic documents of the faith, what we find is that a central admonition of Buddha may be summed up in the words: Do not raise a thirst. As to what goes on in Burma today, nothing is more enlightening than the type of education given to the children of the country by the members of the Buddhist Order. This education consists largely in the memorizing of certain sacred texts. One of the passages especially favored for this purpose, we learn from a recent book on Burma, is Buddha's discussion of the nature of true blessedness, which runs in part as follows:

To wait on mother and father, to cherish child and wife and follow a quiet calling, this is true blessedness.

To give alms, to live religiously, to protect relatives, to perform blameless deeds, this is true blessedness.

To cease from sin, to refrain from intoxicating drinks, to persevere in right conduct, this is true blessedness.

Reverence and humility, contentment and gratitude,

the hearing of the Law of righteousness at fitting moments, this is true blessedness.

Penance and chastity, discernment of the noble truths and the realization of peace, this is true blessedness.

The author of the book on Burma proffers the further information that, as a result of memorizing such verses, the children acquire 'boundless charity and rigid self-control' — a statement one is inclined to receive with some scepticism. Like Kipling, though in an entirely different way, he is probably substituting an idyllic for the real Burma. If only a fraction of what he says is true, we should seek to divert the attention of our own children from radios and motion pictures and set them to memorizing Buddhist verses!

III

The idea that more than any other may be said to have dominated India from remote antiquity is that of yoga (related etymologically to Latin *jugum*, our 'yoke'). Buddha himself has been called the great yogi. Yoga, or the art of 'yoking' one's self, implies a special form of effort put forth in meditation — spiritual strenuousness, as one may say.

Asoka, the Buddhist ruler of India (third century B.C.), though a man of action in every sense, had primarily this form of strenuousness in mind when he had carved on rocks and pillars at various points throughout his vast empire exhortations like the following: 'Let all joy be in effort.' 'Let small and great exert themselves.' In thus admonishing his subjects he aimed to promote, not merely a humanistic wisdom, but saintliness. There are to be sure saints and saints. A few years ago the London papers printed the following dispatch from India: 'A new saint has appeared in the Swāt Valley. The police are after him.' But Asoka's idea of the saint was not so very different from that of the Christian. The virtues he recommended are practically identical, as I have pointed out elsewhere, with the 'fruits of the spirit' enumerated by Saint Paul: 'Love, joy, peace, long-suffering, kindness, goodness, faith, mildness, self-control.'

It follows from all I have said that the essential confusion against which one needs to be on one's guard is that between the quality of will put forth by the oriental in meditation and the pantheistic revery of the primitivist. In his *Defense of the West,* a protest against every form of oriental influence, M. Henri Massis inquires: 'Can there not be found in Bergsonism an attitude analogous to that of the Hindu yogis?' Most emphatically no, I should reply. Yoga, if genuine, is at the opposite pole from the *élan vital* of Bergson. On the other hand, M. Massis is justified in discovering a primitivistic element in Rabindranath Tagore, who, he says, 'denounces the misdeeds of the machinery and technique of the West in the same tone in which Rousseau condemned the corruption of Athens, the decadence of Rome, and the humanism of the Renaissance, in order to exalt the Scythians, the early Persians, and the Germans of Tacitus.' Tagore has genuinely oriental traits, but in his total outlook on life he reminds one less of the ancient sages of his race than of Shelley or even of Maurice Maeterlinck. In short, he must be judged primarily as a romantic poet and as such he has real merits, especially, I am told, in his native Bengali. Is Gandhi again a true Mahatma in the traditonal Hindu sense or is he rather a Tolstoyan utopist? There is room here for hesitation. It must be admitted that Gandhi reminds one in some respects of the traditional Mahatma, but the side of his character and influence that relates him to Tolstoy and ultimately to Rousseau [1] would seem to be the more significant. Like Tolstoy he indulges in an especially vicious confusion between the things of God and the things of Cæsar, a confusion that is no more Buddhist than it is Christian. Buddha once rebuked a group of his followers for even talking about politics. Gandhi would appear to be most utopian in his assumption that his particular mixture of religion and political agitation is compatible with a program of 'non-violence.' One can well understand his horror when he was confronted with the practical outcome of his own dream in the bloody rioting at Bombay in 1921.[2] According to André Siegfried, Europe, appalled by the American excess

[1] This filiation has been traced by Milan I. Markovitch in two volumes: *Rousseau et Tolstoï* and *Tolstoï et Gandhi* (1929). Apropos of these volumes, A. Foucher, professor of Sanscrit at the Sorbonne, wrote me as follows: 'It results from this investigation, based on the documents, that our friend Jean-Jacques has infected even India, and that, in the present conflict between East and West, it is after all the West which has supplied the rods with which it is being beaten. May Heaven preserve us from wouldbe prophets and saints and bestow upon us sages endowed with the sense of measure!'

[2] See *Mahatma Gandhi's Ideas*, by C. F. Andrews (Macmillan, 1930), p. 276.

of standardization and mass production, is tempted to turn from Henry Ford to Gandhi. Before making any such choice, Europe would do well to be less one-sided in its view of America, and also less naïve and uncritical in its notion of what is genuinely oriental in the Orient.

The whole subject is, as a matter of fact, full of pitfalls. Not only has Rousseauistic romanticism had an important influence in the East, but the Orient has had a primitivistic movement of its own deriving from Lao-tze, Chuang-tze, and the early Chinese Taoists. Taoism, if we are to believe M. Massis, has made since the War a strong appeal to German intellectual youth. The main cultural trends of the Far East will be found to go back either to the primitivistic Lao-tze or the humanistic Confucius or the religious Buddha. In tracing these trends one needs to join the utmost keenness of discrimination to fulness of historical knowledge. For not only has each of the three doctrines gone through various phases in itself, but there have been overlappings. In the case of Buddhism, for example, the Great Vehicle (*Mahāyāna*) is not to be judged in the same way as the Small Vehicle (*Hīn-*

ayāna). One needs, furthermore, to distinguish between different branches of Mahāyāna. Take for instance the Zen Buddhism still flourishing in Japan. It is supposed to be close to the genuine teaching of Buddha because the very word Zen implies that it is 'meditative.' [1] But Zen seems to me (perhaps erroneously) to have in it a strong Taoist infusion. Practically this means that the Zenist is more pantheistic and less dualistic in his meditation, or, what amounts to the same thing, less spiritually strenuous than the true Buddhist. What is involved at bottom is the problem of the higher will, a will that is felt in relation to man's ordinary expansive self as a will to refrain, and finally as a will to renounce. The fruit of this renunciation is peace. The various 'return to nature' movements in both East and West have been more or less at the expense of this quality of will. The issue is raised in an especially acute form by the early Chinese Taoists — by Chuang-tze [2] perhaps even more than by Lao-tze himself. They were for getting rid of action

[1] Zen is the Chan Buddhism of China; the word derives ultimately from Sanscrit *Dhyāna* (meditation).

[2] See the article *Chuang-tze as a Romantic*, by Ping-ho Kuo, in the *Sewanee Review* (July, 1931).

in favor of sheer inaction (*Wu Wei*). According to
Professor Kuang-ti Mei of the Chinese Department
at Harvard, 'to the civilized principles of benevo-
lence, righteousness, decorum, knowledge and loy-
alty, the Taoists oppose, like all other primitivists,
heart, nature, natural goodness, instinct, inaction,
silence, unconsciousness, etc. These are the incan-
tations whereby they seek to conjure up their lost
Arcadia.' It must be granted that oriental primitivists have, like Wordsworth and other apostles of
a 'wise passiveness' in the Occident, produced art
and literature of no mean merit. The question may
nevertheless be raised — I have indeed heard it
raised by Chinese themselves — whether Wu Wei
has not had a debilitating effect on Chinese character even to the present day.

That the opposite of outer action is not inaction
but inner action is affirmed in what we have reason
to think a very ancient and authentic passage of the
Buddhist scriptures. On one occasion Buddha
asked alms of a rich Brahmin farmer near Benares
(the work of the farmer has been throughout the
ages the typical form of outer action). This particular farmer seems to have held a view of mendi-

cant friars similar to Voltaire's — namely, that
they had made a vow to God to live at our expense.
'I,' he said to Buddha, 'having ploughed and
sowed, eat. You, on the other hand, propose to eat
without ploughing and sowing.' Whereupon the
Exalted One replied that he was engaged in an even
more important tillage of the spirit. 'Faith is the
seed, penance the rain, understanding my yoke and
plough, modesty the pole of the plough, mind the
tie, thoughtfulness my ploughshare and goad....
Exertion is my beast of burden carrying me without
turning back to the place where, having gone, one
does not grieve. — So this ploughing is ploughed;
it bears the fruit of immortality.'

IV

'Emerson's energetic protests against the Buddhists,' says M. Denis Saurat in a review of the
volume by Dr. Carpenter to which I have already
alluded, 'seem to show that, when he understood
the real meaning of Indian thought, he rejected it
violently, as any normal European or American
does.' It is true that the 'normal European or
American' will not hear of renunciation in its Bud-

[256]

dhist form. It is not clear that he is any more ready
to accept it in its Christian form. A remarkable
feature of the modern man indeed is that he does
not propose to renounce anything and at the same
time hopes to achieve the peace and brotherhood
that are, according to a Buddha or a Christ, to be
achieved only by renunciation. If these great religious teachers should turn out to be right, it follows that what one finds when one penetrates beneath the surface of our contemporary life is a
monstrous huddle of incompatible desires.

The idea of inner action is not merely religious; it
is also humanistic. It is at the basis of true media-
tion as well as of true meditation. It cannot be gain-
said that in its religious form inner action has had
its chief representatives in Asia. There has been
reason in the past, at least, for speaking of the
meditative East. So far from being meditative, we
of the West cannot apparently even grasp the idea
of meditation. Papini, for example, the author of a
life of Christ, discovers the true counterpoise to
what he terms the 'exhausting mercantile super-
stition of our day' in the Wu Wei of the early
Taoists, which he proceeds to equate, not only with

the teaching of Rousseau, but with 'Christian super-wisdom.' Papini evidently supposes that when Christ preferred the wisdom of Mary to that of Martha it was because Mary was loafing and inviting her soul. At the opposite extreme one finds Mr. Bruce Barton's *The Man Nobody Knows*. Mr. Barton tends to present Christ as a precursor of the modern man of business, an apostle of outer action, and even as a go-getter.

The elimination of what one may term the oriental element from Christianity is to be sure nothing new. Dante speaks of the wisdom that a man may win by sitting in quiet recollection. But long before Dante this genuinely religious attitude had been giving way to the crusading spirit. The interpretation of God's will at the Council of Clermont (A.D. 1095) in terms not of inner but of outer action — in this case as a behest to go forth and slaughter Saracens — marks the beginning of a major revolution. Nowadays the crusading, one scarcely needs add, is as a rule not in the name of God but of humanity. One wonders what meaning an American 'uplifter,' who at the same time professes to be a Christian, can attach to such sayings of Christ as 'My peace I give unto you.'

To make another contemporary application of the distinctions I have been attempting, what are we to think of Soviet Russia in its relation to the Orient? It has been said of Stalin in particular that he is Asiatic rather than European in his outlook. There is no doubt an element of truth in the saying 'Scratch a Russian and you will find a Tartar.' One may also grant that autocrats of the Stalin type have been seen in Asia — especially in barbaric Asia. The point that deserves emphasis, however, is that Stalin is using his autocratic power to further something almost inconceivably remote from anything known to the Asia of the past, namely, Marxian materialism. Much that has passed as an expression of the Russian 'soul' is, according to Jules Lemaître, only the Kalmuck exaggeration of French romantic ideas. In much the same way the economic and deterministic explanation of history proclaimed by the Bolsheviks is only the Kalmuck exaggeration of the pseudo-science of the West.

Emotional romanticism and pseudo-science enter

in varying proportions into the nationalism as well as the internationalism that have been sweeping Asia of late, and which are both more or less in conflict with its great traditions. Whatever notion Gandhi, for instance, may have of his own rôle, practically he has counted as a servant of the new Indian nationalism. If by Asia we mean the Asia of Buddha and Confucius and Christ (so far as Christ may be said still to have an Asiatic following), it has more reason to be alarmed at the present occidental invasion than Europe has, according to M. Massis, to be apprehensive of the corrupting influence of the East.

One should remember that the nationalism and internationalism of which I have been speaking are also of comparatively recent origin in the Occident and are likewise in conflict with much that it has held traditionally. Quite apart from tradition and purely as a matter of psychological analysis the underlying opposition in all this clash of tendencies is that between those who affirm in some form the inner life and those who corrupt or deny it. Among the latter are those from Rousseau to Lenin who have discredited the higher will on which the inner life finally depends by their transfer of the struggle between good and evil from the heart of the individual to society. The higher will may be exercised, as I have said, on either the humanistic or the religious level. The humanistic form of the inner life seems to me to have a validity apart from religion (especially if by religion one means some theological formulation of the ultimate mysteries) far greater than Mr. Chesterton and others are willing to concede. Though Asia has much to offer the humanist in its Confucian lore, its superlative achievement, I have been trying to make clear, is to have produced a Christ and a Buddha. One may therefore conclude, waiving for the moment the debate as to the relative claims of humanism and religion as well as innumerable other subsidiary distinctions and disagreements, that there is a choice to be made, as a matter of first principles, between what Christ and Buddha, interpreted in their true spirit and without romantic distortion, represent, and all that is summed up in figures like Rousseau and Lenin. This choice, though it concerns primarily the inner life of the individual, will be found to involve finally all the main issues of civilization.

INDEX OF NAMES

[263]

INDEX OF NAMES

[264]

INDEX OF NAMES

[265]

INDEX OF NAMES